ESSENTIAL

European Community Law

Titles in the series:

ESSENTIAL

European Community Law

by

Richard Owen, LLB, Solicitor
Senior Lecturer
Swansea Law School

First published in Great Britain 1995 by Cavendish Publishing Limited, The Glass House, Wharton Street, London WC1X 9PX

Telephone: 0171-278 8000   Facsimile: 0171-278 8080

British Library Cataloguing in Publication Data

Owen, Richard
Essential EC Law –
(Essential Law Series)
I Title II Series
341.2422

ISBN 1-85941-120-7
Printed and bound in Great Britain

Foreword

This book is part of the Cavendish Essential series. The books in the series are designed to provide useful revision aids for the hard-pressed student. They are not, of course, intended to be substitutes for more detailed treatises. Other textbooks in the Cavendish portfolio must supply these gaps.

Each book in the series follows a uniform format of a checklist of the areas covered in each chapter, expanded treatment of 'Essential' issues looking at examination topics in depth, followed by 'Revision Notes' for self-assessment.

The team of authors bring a wealth of lecturing and examining experience to the task in hand. Many of us can even recall what it was like to face law examinations!

Professor Nicholas Bourne
General Editor, Essential Series
Swansea Law School

Summer 1994

Preface

This book is intended as a revision aid for students studying for degree examinations in EC law. Space is limited and I have tried to concentrate on summaries of academic articles, cases and legislation which students might find particularly useful in the run up to examinations.

Finally, I would just like to say to Liz, Rhodri *bach*, Nest, Griff, Anne, Keith, Marnah and Maureen: *diolch o galon am eich cefnogaeth*.

The law is stated as at 1 September 1994.

Richard Owen

Table of contents

economies sector by sector. A criticism of this approach is that it is an unnatural operation because the integrated sector retains indissoluble links with the other sectors of the economy which still have their national character. Its justification is that it is a first step and is to be followed by the integration of other sectors of the economy until the whole economy is eventually integrated.

An innovative feature of the ECSC Treaty was the creation of four supra national institutions:

- Council of Ministers – representing the Member States;
- High Authority – intended as a supra national executive consisting of independent individuals rather than government representatives, empowered to take legally binding decisions and to procure funds, fix maximum and minimum prices for certain products and fine businesses in breach of competition rules;
- Assembly – a parliament composed of delegates appointed by respective Parliaments of the Member States;
- Court of Justice – to review the legality of the Acts of the High Authority or in some case businesses.

European Atomic Energy Community Treaty (EURATOM)

Established by a Treaty of Rome 1957 the purpose of EURATOM was to create a specialist market for atomic energy, distribute it through the Community, develop nuclear energy and sell surplus to non-Community States.

It set itself the following goals:

- to promote research and ensure dissemination of technical information throughout the Community;
- establish uniform safety standards to protect workers and the general public;
- promote investment in the nuclear energy industry;
- maintain regular and reliable supplies of ores and nuclear fuels;
- make certain that nuclear materials are not diverted for aims other than peaceful purposes.

EURATOM had its own Commission (which was the equivalent to the ECSC's High Authority) and Council of Ministers but shared an Assembly and Court of Justice with the European Coal and Steel Community and European Economic Community. EURATOM is another example of sectoral or functional integration.

European Economic Community Treaty (now EC Treaty)

The European Economic Community (now known as the European Community) was established by a separate Treaty of Rome to EURATOM in 1957 and its name was amended to the EC Treaty by the TEU. The aim in the preamble was, 'to lay the foundations of an ever closer union among the peoples of Europe'.

It set itself the following objectives:

- harmonious development of economic policies;
- continuous and balanced expansion;
- increase in stability;
- accelerated raising of the standard of living;
- closer relations between States.

These objectives have since been amended to the following:

- harmonious and balanced expansion of economic policies;
- sustainable and non-inflationary growth respecting the environment;
- a high degree of convergence of economic performance;
- a high level of employment and social protection;
- the raising of the standard of living and quality of life;
- economic and social cohesion and solidarity among Member States.

The establishment of a common market and the progressive approximation of economic policies of Member States were established to achieve these objectives. Approximation of economic policies has now been changed to an economic and monetary union.

The Community set itself the following goals:

- elimination between Member States of customs duties and quantitative restrictions on import and export of goods and all measures having equivalent effect;
- a common customs tariff and common commercial policy towards third countries;
- abolition between Member States of obstacles to movement of goods, persons, services and capital;
- creation of a common agricultural policy;
- creation of a common transport policy;
- creation of a Community competition policy;
- approximation of laws of Member States to the extent necessary for the functioning of a common market;
- creation of a European Social Fund to improve employment opportunities for workers;

- establishment of a European Investment Bank to facilitate the economic expansion of the Community;
- association of overseas countries and territories to increase trade and promote economic development.

These activities have been added to by later treaties, to include:

- a common commercial policy;
- measures concerning entry and movement of persons;
- a common agricultural and fisheries policy;
- a system ensuring competition is not distorted;
- a policy in the social sphere comprising a European Social Fund;
- the strengthening of economic and social cohesion;
- a policy in the sphere of the environment;
- the strengthening of the competitiveness of Community industry;
- promotion of research and technological development;
- encouragement and establishment of trans-European networks;
- a contribution to the attainment of a high level of health protection;
- a contribution to education and training of quality and flowering of cultures of Member States;
- a policy in sphere of development co-operation;
- association of overseas countries and territories in order to increase trade and promote jointly economic and social development;
- a contribution to the strengthening of consumer protection;
- measures in sphere of energy, civil protection and tourism.

In order to achieve economic and monetary union, the Treaty on European Union added the following activities in the economic field:

- adoption of economic policy based on the close co-ordination of Member States' economic policies;
- on the internal market and on the definition of common objectives, conducted in accordance with the principle of an open market economy with free competition;
- irrevocable fixing of exchange rates leading to a single currency;
- the ECU;
- definition and conduct of a single monetary policy and exchange rate policy;
- support for the general economic policies in the Community.

These activities shall ensure compliance with the following principles:

- stable prices;
- sound public finances and monetary conditions;
- a sustainable balance of payments.

The EEC had its own separate Commission and Council of Ministers but it shared an Assembly and Court of Justice with EURATOM and the ECSC.

The Treaty of Rome embodied a very different approach to integration from the ECSC and EURATOM Treaties. Whereby the latter attempted to integrate sector by sector, the EEC Treaty concentrates on types of activity rather than particular industries (with the exception of agriculture and transport) and aims to ensure the effective functioning of the market together with free and fair competition. Another characteristic of the Treaty of Rome is that it laid down general principles which are left to the Institutions to work out in detailed measures. Policy making and regulation are left to the Institutions. Timetables were laid down for the elimination of mutual trade barriers and a common external tariff. Through these methods the founders hoped to achieve economic integration which was intended to be the forerunner of political integration. The Treaty was intended as a first step, to be followed by later Treaties which would build on the progress made.

Merger Treaty

The three different communities had created three different sets of institutions, although they shared the same Assembly and Court of Justice. It became inconvenient to have three different sets of institutions so a Merger Treaty came into force in 1967. The three communities themselves did not merge (and have still failed to do so) but the High Authority and two Commissions merged to form a single Commission and the three Councils merged to form a single Council. Hartley uses the analogy of three commercial companies with the same shareholders and same board of directors. In law, there are three legal persons, in reality there is only one.

The most important features of the Merger Treaty have been incorporated into the EC Treaty by the Treaty on European Union.

Single European Act

This was the first major amendment to the EC Treaty. It came about as a result of pressure for increased union and also concern over increased competition form North America and the Far East.

The major amendments were, as follows:

- inauguration of the internal market programme for completion by 31 December 1992;
- introduction of majority voting in the Council of Ministers for the enactment of certain measures;

- change in the implementing powers of the Commission;
- creation of a co-operation procedure for the participation of European Parliament in the legislative process;
- recognition of the European Council as a formal organ of the European Community;
- authority granted to the Council of Ministers to create the Court of First Instance;
- co-operation in the field of foreign policy through European political co-operation;
- co-operation in economic and monetary policy;
- common policy for the environment;
- measures to ensure the economic and social cohesion of the Community;
- harmonisation in the fields of health, safety, consumer protection, academic, professional and vocational qualifications, public procurement, VAT & Excise duties and frontier controls.

Treaty on European Union

The most recent amendment to the EC Treaty has been the Maastricht Treaty (officially known as the Treaty on European Union). The TEU creates a European Union with three pillars of the European Community, common foreign and security policy, home affairs and justice policy.

Common foreign and security policy

The key objectives of common foreign and security policy are:

- to safeguard the common values, fundamental interests and independence of the European Union;
- to strengthen the security of the Union and its Member States;
- to preserve peace and strengthen international security in accordance with the United Nations Charter and the Helsinki Act;
- to promote international co-operation;
- to develop and consolidate democracy, the rule of law and respect for human rights and fundamental freedoms;
- for the European Council to define the general policy guidelines. The Council of Ministers will normally take decisions unanimously but will define those matters where qualified majority voting can be used;
- for decisions with defence implications, the European Union will ask for the help of the Western European Union to implement them.

Justice and home affairs

The Member States have defined eight areas of common interest:

- asylum policy;
- crossing of the Community's internal borders;
- immigration policy;
- combating drug addiction;
- judicial co-operation in civil and criminal matters;
- customs co-operation;
- police co-operation;
- joint positions and joint action can be taken by the Council, which can decide certain measures may be adopted by a qualified majority.

General principles

The Treaty on European Union has provisions on three matters of constitutional importance these are human rights, subsidiarity (which is discussed in more detail in Chapter 2) and citizenship.

Human rights

Article F(2) enshrines the existing practice that fundamental rights are to be a general principle of Community law.

Citizenship

Every national of a Member State is to become a citizen of the European Union. This entitles the citizen to:

- reside and move freely around the Union;
- to vote and stand as a candidate in local and European Parliament elections in whichever Member State a citizen resides;
- the right to bring complaints about maladministration by Community institutions before an Ombudsman.

Economic and Monetary Union

The Treaty sets out the procedure and timetable for creating Economic and Monetary Union (EMU).

Stage 1 begins on 1 July 1990. Action is taken to improve co-operation and co-ordination between Member States in economic and monetary fields, strengthen the European Monetary System and the role of the ECU and extend the work of the Committee of Governors of the Member States' central banks.

Stage 2 begins on 1 January 1994 with the establishment of a European Monetary Institute (EMI) promoting co-ordination of Member States' economic policy to bring about EMU. The Commission and the EMI will report on progress of Member States towards convergence. The findings will go to the European Council which will decide whether a majority of States have met the four convergence criteria.

Stage 3 may begin on 31 December 1996 if the European Council takes a qualified majority decision that enough Member States have met the criteria to form a 'critical mass' to move forward to monetary union. The date for completion would then be fixed.

If monetary union has not already formed a European Central Bank (ECB) and a European System of Central Banks would begin in 1998.

If, by the end of 1997, the date set for the beginning of Stage 3 had not already been set, it would begin irrevocably on 1 January 1999 *for those who met the criteria*.

Other changes

The TEU introduces a number of other changes:

- establishes a committee of regions;
- Court of Auditors becomes a Community institution;
- greater powers for the European Parliament, with the introduction of a new legislative procedure;
- greater co-operation in the fields of culture, education, vocational training and youth;
- the Community will play a role in co-ordinating and liaising between Member States on health care programmes and to raise levels of health protection;
- Community will continue to play a role in consumer protection;
- Community will contribute to the development of trans-European networks;
- Community and Member States will co-ordinate their research and development activities;
- Community shall take action leading to social and economic cohesion;
- the Community shall take the environmental aspects laid down in the SEA further by increasing its objectives;
- reaffirmation of the Community's commitment to integrating the economies of the developing nations into the world economy;
- total free movement of capital between Member States and third countries;
- international rules relating to international transport.

Social protocol

Eleven of the Member States have agreed to implement the 1989 European Social Charter, the agreement is annexed to a protocol on social policy which is annexed to the EC Treaty.

The main aims of the social chapter are, as follows:

- supplementing the existing provisions in the social area;
- implementing measures to take into account diverse national practices, in particular in the field of contractual relations and the need to maintain competitiveness;
- supporting and complementing member' activities in the field of workers' health and safety, working conditions, informing and consulting workers, equal opportunity and treatment and integration of people excluded from the labour market and the reinforcement of rules of equal pay.

Opt outs

The TEU contains a number of opt outs:

- Denmark has been given a permanent derogation form Treaty provisions with regard to its second home legislation;
- Ireland has a right to derogate from the Treaty in order to protect the anti abortion provisions of its constitution;
- UK can opt out from the third stage of the EMU;
- UK has opted out of the agreement annexed to the social policy protocol.

The Treaty on European Union has been described as a 'Europe of bits and pieces' by Curtin 30 (1993) CMLRev 17. This refers to the lack of unity contained in the Treaty. The common foreign and security policy, justice and home affairs pillars of the Union use a different institutional structure to the European Communities which contributes to the lack of overall coherence of the Treaty.

Another characteristic of the Treaty is the influence of vested interests which have had an effect upon the outcome. This is evident from the number of opt outs which are contained within the Treaty. The legal significance of this is considered in Chapter 7.

Curtin also criticises the manner in which the Treaty ignores the rights that have been granted to individuals under the European legal order and the way in which the Treaty adds to the lack of transparency in the decision making process.

Other types of acts between Member States

There are two other types of acts between the Member States; subsidiary conventions and acts of the representatives of the Member States.

Subsidiary conventions

Article 220 provides that Member States ought to negotiate conventions to secure, for the benefit of their nationals, the protection of rights, abolition of double taxation, mutual recognition of companies and reciprocal recognition and enforcement of judgments of municipal courts and arbitration awards. The Treaty on European Union provides for future conventions on justice and home affairs.

Acts of representatives of Member States

These occur where members of the Council of the European Union meet, not in their capacity as Council members but, as ministers of their respective governments. This type of act has been given great prominence by the TEU.

General principles of Community law

In every legal system the written sources of law do not provide the answer to every problem which appears before the courts. The ECJ has therefore to develop general principles of law to provide a foundation for judgment.

Sources of general principles

The Treaties

The European Court of Justice has declared that a principle laid down in the Treaty is an application of a more general principle which is not laid down in the Treaty. This is then applied in its own right as a general principle of law, eg, Article 6 prohibits discrimination on the ground of nationality between Union citizens; this has been promoted into a general principle of equality which forbids discrimination on any ground.

The Treaties also provide more specific justification for the development of general principles of law.

Article 164

The Court of Justice shall ensure that, in the interpretation and application of the Treaty, the law is observed. Law in this context must mean something over and above the Treaty itself.

Article 173

This lays down the grounds on which a community act may be annulled. One of these grounds is 'infringement of this Treaty or any rule of law relating to its application'. The phrase 'any rule of law' must refer to something other than the Treaty itself.

Article 215(2)

This is concerned with non-contractual liability and provides that the liability of the Community is based on 'the general principles common to the laws of the Member States'.

Principles of the national laws of the Member States

The European Court of Justice has adopted principles of national laws of Member States. It need not be a principle of every Member State. Whatever the origin of the principle, it will be applied by the ECJ as a principle of Community law not national law.

Principles of human rights in International Treaties

The European Court of Justice in the case of *Nold v Commission* (1974) held that the general principle of fundamental rights was also inspired by Treaties on which the Member States have collaborated or on which they are signatories.

Fundamental human rights

Every Member State is a signatory of the European Convention on Human Rights. The commitment of the Union to human rights was enshrined in Article F(2) of the TEU. This was the recognition of a long standing practice of acceptance of fundamental human rights as a general principle of Community law starting with the case of *Stauder v City of Ulm* (1969).

The rights which have been recognised by the ECJ are as follows:

- property rights, although these are not absolute and unqualified (*Nold v Commission* (1974));
- religious rights (*Prais v Council* (1976));
- right to privacy (*National Panasonic (UK) Ltd v Commission* (1980)) although it did not extend to seizing goods for purposes of EC competition law;
- right to client/lawyer privacy (*A M and S Europe v Commission* (1982));
- due process of law (*Musique Diffusion Française SA v Commission* (1984));
- non-retroactivity of criminal law (*R v Kirk* (1984));
- principle of legal review (*Heylens* (1987)).

Despite all these cases, the importance of this principle should not be overestimated. There has never been a piece of Community law which has been overruled as a result of a human rights provision.

Principle of equality

The EC Treaty has specific examples of equality:

- suppression of discrimination on the ground of nationality (Article 6 (formerly Article 7));
- discrimination between producers and employers of agricultural products is prohibited (Article 40(3));
- discrimination between employees on grounds of sex is prohibited (Article 119).

The European Court of Justice has taken these specific examples and deduced from them a general principle of equality (*Frilli* (1972)).

The principle of equality means that persons in similar situations are not to be treated differently unless the difference in treatment is objectively justified.

Proportionality

This is a principle borrowed from German law. According to this principle a public authority may not impose obligations on a citizen except to the extent to which they are strictly necessary or proportionate to the aim that is being achieved. If a burden is out of proportion then the measure will be annulled. Although the concept is unfamiliar to British lawyers it has been compared to 'reasonableness'; the ECJ have used the term 'reasonableness' on occasion.

Legal certainty

Certainty is a part of most legal systems but in Community law an important concept has developed with various sub-concepts such as non-retroactivity, vested rights and legitimate expectations.

Non-retroactivity and 'vested rights'

The concept of vested rights is often no more than another aspect of retroactivity but it also refers to such matters as the rule of law and the independence of the judiciary. They are rights acquired within the society's legal framework and under due process. The idea is that at any given time a person should know his legal position and his rights should not be taken away by retrospective legislation.

There are two rules relating to non-retroactivity. Firstly, legislation is interpreted with a presumption that it is intended not to have a retrospective effect. Secondly, although there is a general rule which prevents retroactivity, it is allowed where the purpose of a measure would be defeated provided legitimate expectations are respected.

Legitimate expectations

This is another concept which has been borrowed from German law. It was first applied in *Commission v Council 'First staff salaries'* case (1973). The Council had agreed a pay formula which was to last for three years for Commission staff; before the three years had expired the Council attempted to impose a new formula It was held that the new pay scales were invalid as they infringed legitimate expectations.

The principle will not apply if the applicant is acting outside the ordinary course of business. In *EVGF v Mackprang* (1975) the applicant bought grain in France and sold it in Germany to take advantage of a devaluation in the French franc. There was no infringement of legitimate expectations when the Commission authorised German authorities to buy only German grain, as the applicant's actions were purely speculative.

The claimant must also prove not only that he had a legitimate expectation but that there was a causal link between this and his loss (*CNTA v Commission* (1974)).

Legal professional privilege

It was recognised in *A M and S v Commission* (1979) that confidentiality of written communications between lawyer and client was a general principle of Community law but it was subject to two conditions. Firstly, the communication must be for the client's defence, and secondly, the lawyer must be in private practice.

It was held in *National Panasonic (UK) Ltd v Commission* (1980) that there was no violation of a right to privacy if it serves to thwart the enforcement of Community competition law.

Due process and natural justice

This principle has been drawn from English law and requires the making and enforcement of rules of conduct to comply with due process. For example, it was held in *Transocean Marine Paint Association v Commission* (1974) that where a person's interests are affected by a decision of a public authority that person must be given the opportunity to make his views known before the decision is taken.

Equity

The European Court of Justice has also recognised other principles which can conveniently be lumped together under the heading of equity:

- good faith;
- fairness;
- *force majeure.*

Agreements with third countries

The European Court of Justice applies agreements with third countries as an integral part of Community law. There are three types of agreement:

- agreements between the Community and one or more third country;
- 'mixed' agreements between the Community and Member States on the one hand and third countries on the other;
- agreements between Member States and third countries which are only part of Community law in exceptional circumstances.

Legislative Acts

The EC Treaty defines three types of legally binding acts:

- regulations;
- directives;
- decisions.

It also includes recommendations and opinions as two non-legally binding acts.

Regulations

Article 189 provides that regulations have general application. They are also binding in their entirety and directly applicable in all Member States. As to the meaning of 'direct applicability' see Chapter 2.

Regulations help ensure uniformity of law throughout the EC. They are normative in character and will apply generally or to groups of people identifiable in the abstract.

Directives

Article 189 provides that directives are binding 'as to the result to be achieved'. They are binding on the Member States and do not bind individuals until they have been transposed into national law. Although they are binding on the Member States the choice of form and methods when transposing them into national law is left to the national authorities. The purpose of directives is to set a common aim for the Member States. The Member States can then use the most appropriate methods for achieving this aim for their own legal system.

Decisions

Article 189 provides that decisions are binding on those to whom they are addressed. They can be addressed to individual Member States, corporations or private individuals. They differ from regulations, in that they personally point at people as opposed to applying to people or groups in the abstract.

Recommendations and opinions

Recommendations and opinions have no binding force and are of persuasive authority only. In *Grimaldi v Fonds des Maladies Professionnelles* (1989) the ECJ said that national courts are:

... bound to take recommendations into consideration in deciding disputes submitted to them, in particular where they clarify the interpretation of national provisions adopted in order to implement them or where they are designed to supplement binding EEC measures.

Problems with classification of legal acts

It was held in *Confédération Nationale des Producteurs de Fruits et Légumes v Council* (1962) that the legal classification of a legislative act will depend on its substance rather than its form. An act can be called a regulation but if in substance it is a decision it will be treated as such. Consequently, in *International Fruit Co NV v Commission (No 1)* (1970) what was termed a 'regulation' was, in fact, many decisions.

Article 189 envisages distinctive roles for each of the different types of legislative acts. In practice, however, the different acts have been blurred. The ECJ has ruled that directives and decisions have direct effect which makes them less distinct from regulations than one would suppose from a casual reading of Article 189. Directives have often been very detailed when their function was to set an aim which would be fulfilled through national implementing legislation. If the directive is highly detailed then the Member State is not left with much discretion to frame the legislation in the most appropriate way to coincide with its own legal order.

It has been found that some legislative acts are 'hybrids' and are in part a regulation and in part a decision *per* AG Warner in *NTN Toyo Bearing Co Ltd v Council* (1977).

The list of acts contained in Article 189 is not exhaustive. The ECJ has held that other types of act are legally binding, for example, in *Les Verts v European Parliament* (1986) a decision of the Bureau of the European Parliament relating to the distribution of funds prior to the 1984 direct elections was held to be a legally binding act.

Soft law

Soft law is the term used for a measure which is not legally binding but may nevertheless have a practical effect. This type of measure is increasingly prevalent in EC law. For example, recommendations have no legally binding force according to Article 189 but the ECJ said that account must be taken when considering disputes.

The Commission has used soft law in order to achieve its internal market programme through the use of communications, which have been used to explain the implications of ECJ judgments for national governments and private individuals. The practical effect for the Commission is that they are proactive, the Commission is the first to release its interpretation of the ECJ's decision this then sets the agenda for future discussion. In the words of Snyder 56 MLR 19 it '... [provides] guidelines for negotiating the effectiveness of Community law'.

Legal basis

Article 190 requires that each legally binding act contain a statement of reasons on which they are based. The duty to state reasons includes a reference to the legal basis of an act. Prior to the passing of the Single European Act the legal basis of legislation was rarely controversial. Following the SEA the choice of legal basis became more important because it could affect the voting on a proposal which affects the level of influence the Commission can exert over legislation, the choice of legislative procedure and consequently the amount of influence the European Parliament can exert over the passage of the legislation. The Treaty on European Union has further increased the importance of legal basis as it can determine whether legislation is adopted under the EC Treaty or under the Social Policy Protocol from which the UK has opted out; it has introduced new legislative procedures, it has added new competences which are not easy to distinguish from old competences and creates new demarcations between the three pillars of the Union.

Disputes as to legal bases have involved the Court of Justice in inter-institutional conflicts. As the choice of legal base affects the powers of the various institutions, the ECJ effectively adjudicates on the institutional balance within the Community. Emiliou 19 EL Rev 488 describes disputes relating to legal bases, as a form of ' "constitutional" judicial review'. If the Council arrogates to itself too much power by wrongly using a legal base that requires unanimity or restricts the influence of the European Parliament, then the ECJ will intervene to ensure that the correct procedure is followed.

Defects in legal basis can take one of three forms:

- the EC does not have the competence to act;
- the adopting institution does not have the competence;
- the act has been adopted on the wrong basis or no basis has been given.

EC does not have competence

The Treaty on European Union, which includes the the EC Treaty, is a treaty of attribution. The European Union can only act in accordance with the powers and activities which have been laid down in the Treaty. Consequently, the EU is limited to those powers and activities and does not have residual powers as such. A challenge on this ground is very rare.

Lack of competence of adopting institution

The leading case is *France, Italy and United Kingdom v Commission* (1980) which disputed whether the Commission had its own legislative power. The ECJ held that the Commission did have its own legislative power where the Treaty so provides.

Incorrect or unidentified legal basis

Most disputes relating to legal basis have related to an alleged incorrect basis of the legislation. The history of these disputes starts with the passing of the SEA. These disputes started for two reasons. Firstly, it greatly increased the amount of decisions that were to be taken by qualified majority voting. The Commission are keen for decisions to be taken by a qualified majority as opposed to unanimity wherever possible as it increases their influence over the legislation.

The second reason why the SEA increased the importance of legal basis, is that it introduced a new legislative procedure – the co-operation procedure which increases the influence of the European Parliament over the passage of legislation. This procedure is only to be used where specified by the Treaty. The choice of legal basis therefore determines the amount of influence the European Parliament has over the legislation. The TEU introduces another legislative procedure in Article 189b which further increases the Parliament's role. The TEU is also likely to increase disputes relating to legal basis due to the UK's opt out from the Social Policy Protocol. The Working Time Directive 93/104/EC, which limits an employee's working hours, has been adopted by the Council on the basis of Article 118a which allows for harmonisation of health and safety measures. The UK argues that it is not a health and safety measure but a harmonisation of conditions of employment and therefore should be adopted under the Social Policy Protocol. At the time of writing, the measure is being contested before the ECJ. The cases relating to legal bases, therefore, bring to the fore issues relating to the division of power between the Member States and the European Union and also amongst the institutions.

In the *Commission v Council 'Generalised Tariff Preferences'* case (1987) the ECJ said that:

the choice of a legal basis for a measure may not depend simply on an institution's conviction as to the *objective* pursued but must be based on objective factors which are amenable to judicial review.

Many problems have been caused by the more general provisions of the Treaty and their relationship to more specific Treaty provisions, in particular:

- Article 235 which allows the Council, acting unanimously, to take action to achieve a Community objective and the Treaty has not provided the necessary powers to take action.
- Article 100 which allows the Council acting unanimously to issue directives to approximate laws relating to the functioning of the common market.
- Article 100a which allows the Council to issue directives in accordance with the procedure in Article 189b to approximate laws relating to the internal market. Particular problems have been caused by

the relationship of this provision and the environmental protection provisions.

Prior to the introduction of the SEA, the ECJ upheld Article 235 as a legal base in *Hauptzollmat Bremerhaven v Massey-Ferguson* (1973) in the interests of legal certainty. Since this case has been heard qualified majority voting and the co-operation and procedure in Article 189b have been introduced. These developments could explain the ECJ's change of mind in the *Generalised Tariff Preference* case when it said that recourse to Article 235 is justified:

... only where no other provision of the Treaty gives the Community institution the necessary power to adopt the measure in question.

A similar approach has been taken to Article 100. The ECJ in *United Kingdom v Council 'Hormones' case* (1988) held that Article 43, a specific provision, was the appropriate legal base for legislation relating to the production and marketing of agricultural products. Consequently, there was no need to rely on Article 100.

These cases have shown an inclination by the ECJ to insist on reliance on specific provisions at the expense of general provisions, at least in cases where general provisions require unanimity and the specific measures are decided on a qualified majority.

A different approach was taken in *Commission v Council 'Titanium Dioxide' case* (1991). Here the choice was between Article 100a and Article 130s when a directive seemed to pursue dual directives of environmental protection but it also harmonised competitive conditions and therefore also pursued internal market objectives. The ECJ held that the general basis of Article 100a was the correct basis and not the specific powers contained in Article 130s. The roles were reversed in this case as the general power, Article 100a, allowed for majority voting and use of the co-operation procedure while the specific power allowed for unanimous voting and simple consultation with the Parliament. The ECJ made it clear that it was stepping in to determine questions relating to the division of powers between the Community institutions. In particular, it was anxious to safeguard the role of the Parliament in the democratic process.

This approach is hard to reconcile with that used in *Commission v Council 'Waste Directive' case* (1993). Again, a Directive pursued environmental protection and internal market objectives but in this case the ECJ held that Article 130s was the correct base. Internal market measures were very much secondary to environmental matters in this Directive which might help explain the difference in approach.

However, this seems to introduce a subjective approach which has been rejected by the ECJ on previous occasions.

The court seems to have responded to criticism that the *Titanium Dioxide* case threatened to emasculate the Community's environmental policy.

Revision Notes

Sources of law

The main sources of EC law are:

- primary sources: the founding Treaties;
- secondary sources: EC legislation;
- general principles of Community law;
- international agreements with non-Member State;
- decisions of the European Court of Justice.

Primary legislation

ECSC Treaty

The purpose of the Treaty is to create a common market for coal and steel products. Accordingly, certain goals and tasks were set for the Community. Four supra national institutions were created:

- Council of Ministers;
- High Authority (now Commission);
- Assembly (now European Parliament);
- Court of Justice.

EURATOM Treaty

The purpose of this Treaty was to create a specialist market for atomic energy, distribute it through the Community, develop nuclear energy and sell surplus. It set itself certain goals and had its own supra national institutions.

EC Treaty

This Treaty marked a different approach to integration and attempted to integrate types of activity as opposed to sectors of the economy (exceptions being transport and agriculture). The Community set itself certain objectives and means to achieve those objectives, through the creation of a common market and the approximation of economic policies. It also set itself the goals of free movement of the factors of production and a customs union. Economic integration was intended to be the forerunner of political integration.

* The proper functioning of the common market was ensured by free and fair competition and approximation of laws of the Member States.
* The Treaty also provided for the creation of a European Social Fund, European Investment Bank and association agreements with third countries.
* The Community had its own supra national institutions.

Merger Treaty

This merged the Commission and Council of Ministers of the three different institutions. All three communities now have the same institutions.

Single European Act

This was the first major amendment to the EC Treaty. Its main features were the creation of an internal market programme, increased use of majority voting, greater powers for the European Parliament, the European Council was brought within the Community structure, a Court of First Instance was created, greater co-operation in the fields of foreign, economic and monetary policy, a common policy for the environment, measures to ensure social and economic cohesion and harmonisation of laws was extended to new areas.

Treaty on European Union

The most recent amendment to the EC Treaty which created a European Union with three pillars:

* European Community (containing the three communities of ECSC, EURATOM and the EC);
* common foreign and security policy;
* justice and home affairs.

The last two are new areas of intergovernmental co-operation. It has provisions on three areas of constitutional importance:

* human rights;
* subsidiarity;
* citizenship.

Amongst the other changes introduced:

- it sets a timetable for economic and monetary union;
- it also contains a variety of changes on other matters and has a number of opt out clauses.

General principles of Community law

Community law has a number of general principles. The authority for these principles can be found in the following Articles of the Treaty:

- Article 164;
- Article 173;
- Article 215(2).

The other sources for the general principles are principles of the national laws of the Member States and principles of International Treaties on which Member States have collaborated or are signatories.

Fundamental human rights

This is a general principle enshrined in Article F(2) of the TEU. It is drawn from constitutional principles of the Member States and international Treaties on which the Member States have collaborated or are signatories.

Rights which have been recognised are:

- property rights;
- religious rights;
- rights to privacy;
- client-lawyer privacy;
- due process of law;
- non-retroactivity of law;
- legal review.

Principle of Equality

This is a general principle of Community law and includes:

- discrimination on the ground of nationality;
- discrimination between producers;
- discrimination on the ground of sex.

Principle of proportionality

Obligations can only be imposed on a citizen to the extent necessary or proportionate to the aim achieved.

Legal certainty

This can be sub-divided into two different categories:

- non-retroactivity and vested rights;
- legitimate expectations.

Legislative Acts

The EC Treaty defines three types of legally binding acts:

- regulations;
- directives;
- decisions.

Regulations

These apply generally and are directly applicable and ensure uniformity of law.

Directives

These are binding to the result to be achieved. They bind Member States but do not bind individuals until they have been transposed into national law.

Decisions

These are binding on those to whom they are addressed.

Non-legally binding acts

The EC Treaty also provides for non-legally binding acts:

- recommendations;
- opinions.

Although they do not have a binding force national courts must take these non-legally binding acts into account when interpreting national provisions (*Grimaldi v Fonds des Maladies Professionelles* (1988)).

Legal basis

Defects in legal basis can take one of three forms:

* EC does not have competence to act;
* adopting institution does not have competence to act;
* the act is adopted on the wrong basis or none has been given.

The Single European Act and the Treaty on European Union have increased the number of disputes relating to legal basis due to increased powers for the European Parliament and the increase in majority voting.

Most disputes relate to the use of a wrong legal basis. The greatest number of problems relate to the more generalised provisions of Articles 100, 100a and 235.

The European Court of Justice has said that reasons for choice of a certain legal base must be decided on objective grounds. Articles 235 and 100 are similar in the sense that they both require unanimity and the simple consultation procedure. This explains why the ECJ only allows recourse to these provisions; 'where no other provision of the Treaty gives the Community institution the necessary power to adopt the provision in question' (*Generalised Tariff Preference* case (1987) and *Hormones* case (1988)).

Article 100a allows for majority voting and use of the co-operation procedure. The European Court of Justice has been prepared to allow recourse to this provision as a legal base (*Titanium Dioxide* case (1991)). unless the measure only incidentally touches on Article 100a (*Waste Directive* case (1993)). A more subjective element has been used with respect to Article 100a than for Articles 235 and 100.

2 EC law and national law

ESSENTIALS

You should be familiar with the following areas:	✓
• direct effect	
• interpretive obligation (indirect effect)	
• remedies against national governments	
• primacy of EC law	
• subsidiarity	
• preliminary references	

Direct effect

Direct effect of Treaty provisions

Usually international Treaties are agreements between governments and do not create rights for citizens enforceable before national courts.

The Community legal order differs from international law, in this respect, as it creates rights for citizens which are enforceable before national courts, this is what is meant by direct effect.

The concept started with the case of *Van Gend en Loos v Nederlandse Administratie der Belastingen* (1963). A private firm sought to invoke Community law against Dutch customs authorities in proceedings before a Dutch tribunal. A preliminary reference was made to the ECJ.

The Dutch government argued that an infringement of the Treaty did not give an individual the right to bring an action. Actions could only be brought against the government of a Member State by another Member State or by the Commission.

It was held that the Treaties created a 'new legal order' which created rights for individuals which became part of their legal heritage.

Van Gend en Loos was brought on the basis of Article 12, which is a negative obligation as it requires that Member States refrain form introducing any new customs duties on imports and exports.

The concept was extended in the case of *Alfons Lütticke GmbH v Commission* (1966) when it was held that a positive obligation could have direct effect once the time limit for implementation has expired.

The criteria for a provision to have direct effect were set out by Advocate General Mayras in *Reyners v Belgium* (1974), as follows:

- the provision must be clear and unambiguous;
- it must be unconditional;
- its operation must not be dependent on further action being taken by the Community or national authorities.

It can be deduced from this that certain provisions of the Treaty are not directly effective because they are too vague. There must not be any discretion attached to the implementation of the provision nor must the right be dependent on some legislative or executive action of the Commission of a Member State until such action has been taken or the time limit for taking action has expired.

Van Gend en Loos is an example of what is known as vertical direct effect. The obligation rested on an organ of the State and there was a corresponding right on individuals. It was held in *Defrenne v SABENA (No 2)* (1976) that Treaty obligations could be conferred on individuals as well as Member States, so called horizontal direct effect. The applicant was an air stewardess employed by SABENA. She brought an action against them based on Article 119 which provides that men and women shall receive equal pay for equal work. The applicant claimed that male air stewards were paid more for performing exactly the same tasks as stewardesses and this was a breach of Article 119. SABENA argued that the Treaty obligations could not be imposed on private persons as well as the State.

In addition to direct effect there is a principle of 'direct applicability' which means that a provision becomes operative in a Member State immediately without the need for the national legislature to pass implementing legislation to incorporate it into national law.

Certain provisions of the Treaty are directly applicable and there is no need for there to be further legislation by national parliaments incorporating it into national law as it is incorporated already.

The terms direct applicability and direct effect have been used interchangeably by the ECJ, yet they are separate concepts. A provision can be directly applicable in the sense that it forms part of the law of a Member State in the absence of implementing legislation and yet not be sufficiently precise to have direct effect.

Conversely, a Community provision can be sufficiently precise to be relied on before a national court even though it has not been transposed into national law.

Direct effect of regulations

Article 189 states that 'a regulation shall have general application. It shall be binding in its entirety and directly applicable in all Member States'.

As regulations are directly applicable they do not need national implementing legislation. The ECJ have gone further in *Leonesio v Italian Ministry of Agriculture* (1972) when it said that not only is national implementing legislation unnecessary it is illegal.

The ECJ felt that there would be three main dangers if regulations were implemented into national law:

- it would be unclear as to whether they took effect from the date of the national measure or the date of the Community measure;
- there would be subtle changes made to the Regulation when it is transferred to national legislation;
- it could prejudice the ECJ's jurisdiction to give a ruling on the interpretation and validity of the measure under the preliminary reference procedure.

Nevertheless, there are exceptions to the rule that regulations do not need national implementing legislation:

- where the regulation expressly requires national implementing legislation: *Commission v United Kingdom 'Tacograph* case' (1979);
- where a regulation impliedly requires that a Member State brings forward national legislation eg where the terms of a regulation are vague, though the national legislation must not be incompatible with the regulation;
- a third possible area suggested by Hartley is where a Member State wishes to codify the law in a particular area ie draw on all the relevant law on one particular topic into one piece of legislation.

To be directly effective and capable of creating rights for individuals enforceable before national courts, they must satisfy the criteria for direct effectiveness:

- the provision must be clear and unambiguous;
- it must be unconditional;
- its operation must not be dependent on further action being taken by Community or national authorities.

Direct effect of Directives

Article 189 states that directives are 'binding as to the result to be achieved' but that the choice of 'form and methods' is left to the Member State.

In contrast to regulations the Treaty does not make any reference to them being directly effective, they cannot be directly applicable as they require national implementing legislation to give effect to them.

Despite the Treaty being silent on the point, the ECJ held that Directives had direct effect in *Franz Grad v Finanzamt Traunstein* (1970) when a Directive specified the commencement date for a provision and a substantive provision of a Directive was held to have direct effect in *Van Duyn v Home Office* (1974).

The main reasons why the ECJ gave direct effect to Directives were:

* to make them more effective;
* to estop a Member State from relying on its own wrongdoing.

There was a strong reaction against giving direct effect to Directives in the Member States and the French *Conseil d'Etat* and initially the German Federal Tax Court denied that Directives had direct effect.

The ECJ took this reaction into account and in addition to having to satisfy the criteria for direct effect the ECJ has placed two other important limitations on the direct effect of Directives:

* they cannot have direct effect before the time limit for implementation has expired (*Ratti* (1979));
* they do not have horizontal direct effect (*Marshall v Southampton and South West Hampshire AHA (No 1)* (1986)).

A Directive can be directly effective and may be invoked as such, even though it has been transposed into national law (*Verbond van Nederlandse Ondernemingen (VNO) v Inspecteur der Invoerrechten en Accijnzen* (1977)).

The disadvantages of only giving vertical direct effect to Directives are that it restricts the effectiveness of directives within the national legal system, and it prejudices the uniform application of Community law. Also, it discriminates between individuals. For example, in employment law a State employee can rely on a Directive as against an employer whereas a private employer cannot.

Despite these disadvantages, the ECJ once again ruled in *Faccini Dori* (1994) that Directives do not have direct effect.

As a result of these difficulties the ECJ has had to develop various stratagems to circumvent the problems created by this limitation of on the direct effect of Directives. One of these stratagems has been to widen the definition of the State to enable as many employees as possible to rely on Directives.

Organ of the State

In *Marshall (No 1)* the UK argued that where the State was acting as an employer it was no different to a private employer. The ECJ rejected this argument and held that it did not matter in what capacity the State was acting in, Directives could still be relied on against it.

In *Foster v British Gas plc* (1990) it was held that a privatised public utility undertaking was an 'organ of the State' as it was offering a public service under the control of a public authority and therefore had special powers.

While in *Johnston v Chief Constable of the Royal Ulster Constabulary* (1986) it was held that a Directive could be relied on against a Chief Constable as he is responsible for the direction of the police service. As a police authority is charged by the State with the maintenance of public order and safety, it does not act as a private individual. On that basis it could be regarded as an 'organ of the State'.

Direct effect of decisions

Under Article 189 a decision of the Council or Commission is binding on those to whom it is addressed. It can be addressed either to Member States, individuals or corporations.

They were again held in *Franz Grad v Finanzamt Traunstein* (1970) to be directly effective. Again before they can be directly effective they must fulfil the criteria for direct effectiveness.

Direct effect of international agreements

Agreements with non-Member States have been held to be directly effective, even if they are not directly effective in the non-Member State (*Kupferberg* (1982)).

Interpretive obligation (indirect effect)

The main limitations on the direct effect of Directives are that they cannot have horizontal direct effect nor can they have direct effect before the time limit for implementation has expired. These limitations meant that the effectiveness of Directives has been seriously undermined. The ECJ has created an interpretive obligation on the national courts when interpreting national legislation which to some extent circumvents these restrictions indirectly.

The origins of the obligation are seen in the case of *Von Colson and Kamann v Land Nordrhein-Westfalen* (1984). A German prison refused to employ two women social workers who were better qualified than the men who were employed in their place. The equal treatment principle had been infringed but the German legislation implementing the Directive limited the right to compensation to a limited nominal sum. The Directive had not specified the form of the sanction for infringement of the equal treatment principle but it was intended to be an adequate remedy. As there was a discretion in the hands of the Member States as to how the sanction was to be implemented, the provision did not fulfil the criteria for direct effect. On a preliminary reference the ECJ used Article 5 which places Member States under an obligation to fulfil their Treaty obligations.

The ECJ said that Article 5 was an obligation addressed to all national authorities which includes national courts. National courts are therefore under an obligation to interpret national legislation in accordance with the aims and purposes of the Directive.

A limitation was placed on the obligation by the ECJ as it said that it only existed 'so far as it was possible' for the national court to give the national legislation a Community interpretation. Another uncertainty created by the case was that it involved legislation which had been introduced to implement the Directive and it was unclear whether the obligation extended to legislation which was not framed with the intention of implementing a directive.

The existence of the obligation was reiterated in *Kolpinghuis Nijmegen BV* (1987) which also added that the obligation existed between the date that the obligation is adopted and the the date of the time limit for its implementation into national law. This raises problems as to legitimate expectations and non-retroactivity. Individuals will have arranged their affairs on the basis of national legislation as it has been implemented and will not have bargained for a re-interpretation which effectively changes the law. In *Kolpinghuis Nijmegen* the ECJ stated that the interpretive obligation was subject to the general principles of legal certainty and non-retroactivity.

The guidelines for the interpretive obligation were recently dramatically extended in the case of *Marleasing SA v La Comercial Internacional de Alimentacion SA* (1992). The plaintiff, Marleasing, sought to set aside the memorandum and articles of association of La Commercial on the grounds that, in the view of the plaintiff, it had been set up to put certain assets beyond the reach of creditors. The First Company Directive 68/55 exhaustively sets out the grounds on which a company can be declared void and does not list fraud. However, the Spanish had not transposed the Directive into their law. Their own Civil Code was enacted before the Directive so could not possibly have been brought forward with the intention of implementing the legislation. Nevertheless, the ECJ in a preliminary reference said that the obligation extended to the Civil Code even though it had been enacted prior to the Directive.

An effect of the ruling was that the plaintiff was able to rely on the Directive against the defendant, even though Directives do not have horizontal direct effect, yet this result was achieved by indirect methods. Interestingly, the ECJ specifically said that *Marshall (No 1)* was good law and that directives do not have horizontal direct effect. Again the ECJ added a qualification to the obligation when they stated that it only existed 'so far as is possible'. A further difficulty was the the ECJ did not state the extent to which the obligation is limited by the general principles of legitimate expectation and non-retroactivity. They had previously stated that these general principles did limit the obligation in relation to criminal cases in *Kolpinghuis Nijmegen* but the situation is unclear in civil cases.

There is currently an academic argument raging as to the significance of *Marleasing*. Writers such as Smith, de Burca, Mercer and Prechal advance arguments that the obligation is extremely wide and that, as a result of the case, virtually all conflicting national provisions will have to be interpreted in accordance with Directives. On the other hand, Maltby says that as the obligation only exists 'so far as is possible' it is a far narrower than the other writers suggest and only exists where there are quite genuinely two possible ways in which to interpret the national legislation, one which accords with the Directive and one which does not. In that situation there is an obligation on the national court to give a Community interpretation.

It is safe to say that the limits placed on the obligation in *Von Colson* and *Marleasing* and the uncertainty surrounding the effect of the general principles of legitimate expectation and non-retroactivity make the scope of the obligation unclear.

The interpretive obligation has the effect of safeguarding the Community rights of those who might otherwise be unable to rely on such rights because of the limitations on the direct effect of Directives laid down in *Marshall (No 1)*. However, as Plaza Martin points out it also has the disadvantage of making the position of defendants uncertain, as they will be unsure as to whether national law needs to be read in the light of the aims and purposes of Community Directives or whether it is safe for them to assume that national law has correctly implemented the Directive.

Interpretive obligation and UK courts

The interpretive obligation has given rise to difficulties in UK courts. The difficulties stem from the doctrine of sovereignty of Parliament which makes British judges reluctant to construe legislation contrary to its ordinary and literal meaning. Initially, the UK courts would interpret domestic law only in the light of directly effective provisions of EC law. This approach was based on a combined reading of s 2(1) and s 2(4) of the European Communities Act 1972, which would seem only to give primacy to directly effective provisions of EC law over UK law. Before *Von Colson* in *Garland v British Rail Engineering Ltd* (1983) the courts used a rule of construction in respect of s 6(4) of the Equal Pay Act which was apparently contrary to Article 119. However, there was an ambiguity in s 6(4) and it was possible to give a Community interpretation to it without an undue straining of the words. This accorded with an established principle of English law that, when interpreting statutes which are intended to implement an obligation contained in an international Treaty and there is an ambiguity, the presumption is that Parliament intended to fulfil the obligation, and the interpretation which accords with the Treaty should be given. In this way it was possible to juggle both Parliamentary sovereignty and give primacy to Community law.

In *Pickstone v Freemans plc* (1987) it was impossible to construe s 1(2)(c) of the Equal Pay Act against its literal meaning in order for it to conform with Article 119. The House of Lords did not attempt to distort the meaning of the Act and instead applied Article 119 directly. Similarly, in *Litster v Forth Dry Dock and Engineering Co Ltd* (1990) the House of Lords read into the Transfer of Undertakings Regulations, which was intended to implement a Directive, a clause which could not be implied from its literal meaning. These cases represent an advance on *Garland* as they show a willingness to give primacy to EC law directly. However, it should be noted that in both cases the British legislation was intended to give effect to Community obligations.

The most controversial decision in this area is *Duke v GEC Reliance Ltd* (1988). The Sex Discrimination Act 1975 did not prohibit discrimination in relation to retirement ages. It was enacted a year before the

Equal Treatment Directive 76/207 which did prohibit such discrimination. The House of Lords refused to interpret the Act in accordance with the Directive as it had clearly not been intended to implement it. Lord Templeman said that the *Von Colson* principle only applied in relation to legislation which was intended to implement a Directive. He also said that *Von Colson* was not an authority for distorting national legislation which did not conform to Community legislation which lacked direct effect.

The decision in *Duke* must now be read in the light of the *Marleasing* decision. De Burca states that it is not compatible with *Marleasing* while Maltby says that it was wrong to assert in *Duke* that it is necessary for the national legislation to come after the Community legislation and be intended to implement it. The interpretive obligation extends to legislation enacted prior to the Community obligation but only exists where there is an ambiguity in the national legislation. It does not, in his view, require national courts to disregard the meaning of national legislation.

Remedies against national governments

In the UK it has been held that infringement by a government department of enforceable Community rights gives rise to a right to judicial review but not to damages (*Bourgoin v MAAF* (1985)).

This is now doubtful as a result of the decision in *Francovich, Bonifaci v Italy* (1992). The applicants had been employees in businesses which became insolvent, leaving substantial arrears of salary unpaid. The Italian government had failed to implement a Directive which had obliged them to set up a compensation scheme to protect employees of insolvent employers. This breach had been proved in enforcement proceedings which had been taken against Italy.

The provisions of the Directive did not have direct effect. Nevertheless, the ECJ held that Article 5 requires Member States to fulfil their Community obligations and that the effectiveness of Community law would be called into question and the the protection of enforceable Community rights would be weakened if individuals could not obtain compensation when their rights were infringed. On this basis it was said to be inherent from the scheme of the Treaty that individuals should receive compensation from the State when a Member State had breached its Community obligations. This right is subject to three conditions:

- the Directive must confer rights on individuals;
- the content of these rights is identifiable by reference to the Directive;
- there is a causal link between the breach of a State's obligation and the damage suffered by the persons affected.

Francovich is obviously a far reaching decision. In the first attempt by a national court to interpret it in *Kirklees Borough Council v Wickes Building Supplies Ltd* (1992) the House of Lords doubted whether *Bourgoin* could be considered good law. Their Lordships said that the liability in damages for breach of a Community obligation rested solely on central government and local authorities could not be responsible in damages for a breach of obligation.

The obligation has been further extended in the case of *Marshall v Southampton and South West Hampshire Area Health Authority (No 2)* (1993). The applicant had been unlawfully discriminated against contrary to Community law. However, the Sex Discrimination Act placed an upper limit on her compensation and did not award interest. The applicant's actual loss was valued at £18, 405 and she challenged these limits.

The ECJ held that Article 6 of the Equal Treatment Directive provides that the Member State must provide a remedy which guarantees real and effective judicial protection and have a deterrent effect when the principle has been infringed. Financial compensation must be such that the loss and damage caused by the breach must be made good in full and interest must be awarded to maintain the value of the loss.

The decision ensures the full and effective protection of directly effective Community rights in national courts. Where a Directive does not have direct effect then the individual may have the full protection of Community rights in damages against the State.

The decision in *Marshall (No 2)* has made a start at solving one of the problems associated with *Francovich* by ensuring that there is uniformity in the *quantum* of damages awarded.

The decision in *Francovich* will also have a deterrent effect on Member States. As Member States now face the possibility of paying substantial damages if they are late in implementing a Directive it will encourage them to act on time. It acts as a penalty on the Member State but this supplements the Member States liability under Article 171 which was amended by the Treaty on European Union so that Member States that fail to comply with judgments which are the end result of enforcement proceedings can now face penalties under that provision as well.

A disadvantage of this deterrent effect of *Francovich* has been identified by Martin as a slowing down of the decision making process with the Member States making sure that Directives are drafted with the utmost care prior to adopting them or alternatively they may go to the other extreme and demand that rights are so vague that they could not be relied on by applicants. Another limitation is that the decision attempts to put the applicant in the position he would have been in had the directive been properly implemented. However, in some cases money can only be an approximate compensation for what has been lost.

The scope of *Francovich* is still unclear and it is uncertain as to whether it applies where a Member State has implemented a Directive *bona fide* on a reasonable interpretation but is shown through an unexpected interpretation by the ECJ that it is mistaken.

Procedural remedies

In addition to the substantive right to damages the ECJ have also ensured the effective protection of Community rights through the creation of effective procedural remedies.

In *R v Secretary of State ex p Factortame Ltd (No 1)* (1990) it was held by the ECJ that where a national court considered that the sole obstacle to granting *interim* relief was a rule of national law then it was obliged to set aside that rule. This ruling has been interpreted as creating a new procedural remedy for the protection of Community rights.

In *Emmott v Minister for Social Welfare* (1991) it was held that where a Directive has not been correctly transposed into national law then time does not start to run for the purpose of limitation periods until the Directive is properly implemented into national law. This right exists even in respect of non-directly effective rights and also in the absence of the ECJ failing to declare that the Member State has failed to fulfil its obligations. In other words, time does not start to run until an individual is certain what his legal rights are.

In *Zuckerfabrik Süderdithmarschen AG v Hauptzollmat Itzehoe* (1991) it was held that the power of a national court to suspend administrative acts which are based on a Community measure whose validity is in doubt can only order a suspension on the same conditions as those applied by the ECJ in *interim* measure proceedings.

Primacy of EC law

'Twin pillars'

The Community legal order is said to be built on the 'twin pillars' of direct effect and supremacy. The case of *Van Gend en Loos v Nederlandse Administratie der Belastingen* (1963) first stated the principle of supremacy when it held that a Treaty provision took priority over a conflicting piece of earlier Dutch legislation. The case is better known for laying the other pillar of the legal order namely the principle of direct effect.

The second pillar of the supremacy of Community law was laid in the case of *Costa v ENEL* (1964). The ECJ held that Community law could not be overridden by domestic legal provisions regardless of whether the provisions came earlier or later than Community law.

The basis of the principle of supremacy was found to arise from the words and spirit of the Treaty rather than in national constitutions, which can be seen from a famous piece of the ECJ's *dicta:*

The transfer by the states from their domestic legal system to the Community legal system of rights and obligations arising under the Treaty carries with it the permanent limitation of their sovereign rights against which a subsequent unilateral act incompatible with the concept of the Community cannot prevail.

The court argued that a restriction of sovereign rights and the creation of a body of law applicable to individuals as well as Member States, made it necessary for this new legal order to override inconsistent provisions of national law. Community law was also prepared to reach into national law and provide remedies where national law did not do so.

Community law overrules provisions of national constitutions

The rule is an unconditional rule and applies to every rule of domestic law whatever its standing. Consequently, Community law cannot be tested in municipal courts for compliance with constitutions of Member States.

In *Internationale Handelsgesellschaft GmbH* (1970) it was held that recourse to the legal rules or concepts of national law in order to judge the validity of measures adopted by the Community would have an adverse effect on the uniformity and efficacy of Community law.

Therefore, the validity of a Community measure or its effect within a Member State cannot be affected by allegations that it runs counter to either fundamental rights as formulated by the constitution of that State or the principles of a national constitutional structure.

Principle of supremacy must be applied immediately

Primacy is a rule which is addressed to the national courts and is to be applied immediately by *every* national court.

In *Administrazione delle Finanze dello Stato v Simmenthal SpA* (1978) an Italian court was faced with a conflict between a Council regulation and Italian laws, some of which were subsequent in time to the Italian regulation. Under Italian law legislation, contrary to EC regulations, can be declared unconstitutional but only by the constitutional court and not by ordinary courts. The Italian judge made a preliminary reference on the question of whether direct applicability of regulations required national courts to disregard inconsistent subsequent national legislation without waiting for relevant legislation to be eliminated by national law.

It was held that every national court must apply Community law in its entirety and must accordingly set aside any provision of national law which may conflict with it.

If national law impairs the effectiveness of Community law by withholding the power to set aside an inconsistent piece of national law, then that rule is contrary to Community law.

Member States cannot plead *force majeure*

A Member State cannot say that it has tried to comply with an obligation or remedy a breach but it has been prevented by legislature from doing so.

In *Commission v Italy 'art treasures case'* (1968) an Italian tax on art treasures was in violation of Italy's obligation under Article 16 to abolish customs duties on exports. The ECJ held that by continuing to levy the tax they were in breach of Community law. Legislation had been introduced but lapsed with the dissolution of the Italian Parliament. The government's inability to to force the legislation through was not an excuse for failing to give effect to the principle of supremacy.

This was followed by *Commission v Italy 'second art treasures case'* (1970) when the Commission took enforcement proceedings against Italy for failing to comply with the 1968 judgment as there had been a delay until late 1971 before the tax was abolished and a refund paid to exporters.

The government argued that the legislation had depended upon the legislature which had been unable to bring forward the legislation. The ECJ held that it was a directly applicable provision which did not need national legislation to give effect to it but the court indicated that the principle was wider than this as the Treaties involved a limitation on sovereign rights which could not be overridden by national law.

Similarly, the court disallowed the claim of a Member State that the payment of a premium for the slaughter of cows under a Community provisions dependent on the adoption of budgetary provisions (*Leonesio v Italian Ministry of Agriculture 'the Slaughtered Cow'* (1972)).

Supremacy applies regardless of nature of rule of law

The principle of supremacy applies irrespective of whether the inconsistent provision of national law has a civil or criminal character (*Procureur du Rou v Dassonville* (1974)).

A Belgian importer imported Scotch Whisky from France in the absence of a certificate of origin from the UK contrary to the Belgian Criminal Code. As the goods had been acquired from a French agent obtaining a certificate of origin would have been expensive and difficult.

The Belgian Criminal Court made a preliminary reference asking whether the provisions of the Treaty provided a defence to the proceedings. The ECJ held proceedings contravened Article 30 and no charges could therefore be brought.

Supremacy applies regardless of source of law

In addition to the principle applying regardless of the character of national law it also applies regardless of the source of national law. Both inconsistent statutes and judicial precedents have been declared inapplicable and also rules of professional bodies may be held inconsistent and applicable (*R v Royal Pharmaceutical Society of Great Britain* (1989)).

Supremacy applies regardless of the form of community law

The principle of supremacy applies to different forms of Community law. Consequently, it will apply whether the Community provision is a Treaty article, a Community act or an agreement with a third country.

Member States must repeal conflicting legislation

Member States are obliged to repeal conflicting national legislation, even though it is not enforced, merely 'inapplicable' (*Commission v France 'French Merchant Seamen'* case (1974)).

A French law provided that a certain proportion of the crew on French merchant ships had to be of French nationality. This was a conflict with Community law and enforcement proceedings were brought against France. The French government argued that the law had not been applied and as it was regarded as inapplicable, France had not violated the Treaty.

The ECJ held that the existence of the law created 'an ambiguous state of affairs' which would make seamen uncertain as to the possibilities available to them of relying on Community law. It was not enough simply not to enforce the law it had to be repealed.

Interpretation of Community law

Member States cannot give authoritative rulings on the interpretation of Community law.

A classic weapon that states use to undermine a Treaty is interpretation. This weapon has been taken away from the Member States as the interpretation of the Treaty has been entrusted to the ECJ under the preliminary reference procedure (see below) but there is a double check because Article 219 provides that:

... the Member States undertake not to submit any dispute concerning the interpretation or application of the Treaty to any method of settlement other than those provided in the Treaty.

This puts the ECJ in a monopolist position.

Indirect or potential conflict

So far, we have looked at situations where there is a direct conflict between the provisions of national law and Community law but the powers of the Member State can be limited even where the conflict is only indirect or potential.

In *Commission v Council (ERTA)* (1971) it was held that Member States could not enter into agreements with non-Member States on matters which were within the competence of the Communities.

This loss of jurisdiction applies even where the conflict is only indirect or potential.

Also, Member States cannot pass national legislation on matters which are within the competence of the Treaties, even in the absence of a direct conflict.

Principle of supremacy and UK law

The British courts faced tremendous difficulties in reconciling the principle of supremacy with British constitutional law. In particular, the courts had to juggle three constitutional conventions of the doctrine of parliamentary sovereignty, the doctrine of implied repeal and the principle that no parliament can bind its successor with the principle of supremacy.

The UK has a dualist constitution and international Treaties will only have the force of law if they have been incorporated into UK law. EC law is incorporated into UK law by virtue of the European Communities (Amendment) Act 1972 which has been amended by the European Communities (Amendment) Act 1986, which incorporated the Single European Act and the European Communities (Amendment) Act 1993 which incorporated the Treaty on European Union. As the UK does not have a written constitution these all have the status of ordinary Acts of Parliament and can therefore be repealed by subsequent parliaments.

The key sections of the 1972 Act are s 2(1) which provides for the direct effect of Community law in the UK. Section 2(2) provides for the implementation of Community law by means of subordinate legislation. Section 2(4), together with s 3(1), in effect provides for the recognition of the principle of supremacy.

The landmark decision with regard to supremacy and UK law is *R v Secretary of State for Transport ex p Factortame Ltd* (1990). The Merchant Shipping Act 1988 was challenged by a group of Spanish fishermen as contrary to Community law. The House of Lords felt that they could not grant interim relief pending the outcome of a preliminary ruling. In their view an Act of Parliament was presumed to comply with Community law until a decision on compatibility had been given. The Court of Justice held that where a national court is hearing a case which involves questions involving Community law and the national court feels that the sole reason preventing it from granting interim relief is a rule of national law, then it must set aside that rule. Consequently, any Act of Parliament passed after the 1972 Act must be read as subject to directly enforceable Community rights. (See also *R v Secretary of State for Transport ex p Factortame (No 2)* (1991)).

Recently in *R v Secretary of State for Employment ex p Equal Opportunities Commission* (1994) the House of Lords rules that rights under the Employment Protection (Consolidation) Act should be extended to part time workers despite Parliament's express intention to the contrary.

Subsidiarity

The principle of subsidiarity was introduced into Community law, in matters relating to the environment, by Single European Act Article 130 r(4):

The Community shall take action relating to the environment to the extent to which the objectives referred to in paragraph 1 can be attained better at Community level than at the level of the individual Member States.

It was made a general principle of Community law by virtue of the Treaty on European Union, Article 3(b) provides:

The Community shall act within the limits of the powers conferred upon it by this Treaty and of the objectives assigned to it therein.

In the areas which do not fall within its exclusive competence, the Community shall take action, in accordance with the principle of subsidiarity, only if and in so far as the objectives of the proposed action cannot be sufficiently achieved by the Member States and can therefore, by reason of the scale of the proposed action, be better achieved by the Community.

Any action by the Community shall not go beyond what is necessary to achieve the objectives of this Treaty.

Is subsidiarity justiciable?

It has been argued that subsidiarity is not a legal principle at all and that the ECJ is not equipped to decide subsidiarity questions which involve economic and political judgments. Emiliou 17 (1992) ELRev 383 says it can only be understood in the context of a federal system.

Toth 19 EL Rev 268 argues that subsidiarity is justiciable, in part. The principle only applies to areas which do not fall within the Community's exclusive competence. The ECJ therefore has a role in ruling whether a matter is within or outside the Community's exclusive competence. In ruling whether something is within or outside exclusive competence, the ECJ will be ruling on whether a matter falls within or outside the principle.

Another suggestion is that the ECJ could restrict itself to a 'marginal review' of subsidiarity. The ECJ would confine itself to deciding whether the discretion is properly exercised by looking to see whether the decision was based on an obvious factual error or constituted a misuse of powers.

Decisions as to the correct legal base can also affect the applicability of the subsidiarity principle. If an act could be adopted on two different legal bases, one of which involves exclusive competence and the other does not, should the ECJ choose the base which involves exclusive competence, then it will have excluded the operation of the subsidiarity principle.

Exclusive jurisdiction and concurrent powers

The subsidiarity principle does not apply to matters which are within the Community's exclusive jurisdiction. At the time of the Treaty on European Union there seemed to be an assumption on the part of some politicians that concurrent powers were somehow jointly exercised by the Member States and the Community and that subsidiarity would have a role in determining whether these powers would be better exercised by the Member States or the Community.

This is a fundamentally mistaken view as to the nature of concurrent powers. If a power is held concurrently then the Member State can act only up to the point at which the Community exercises its rights. Once the Community has acted then it has exclusive jurisdiction and the Member State no longer has jurisdiction to act.

Some writers have found that exclusive competence is a very broad concept, which consequentially means that subsidiarity applies in a narrow area. Toth 29 CML Rev 255 says, 'the EC's competence is exclusive over all matters pertaining to the common objectives'. Therefore, subsidiarity cannot apply to anything contained in the original EEC Treaty, whereas, Steiner takes the view that exclusive competence is limited to those areas where the Community has already legislated.

Does subsidiarity contain competing tests?

The principle of subsidiarity has been criticised for containing inherent competing tests. If the action can be more effectively taken by the Member State then it should be taken at that level (the so called test of effectiveness) but if the scale of the action can be better achieved by the Community it should be taken at that level (so called test of scale). It has been argued that there is an inherent conflict between these two tests. The example has been given of the environment where the patrolling of beaches is clearly an activity which can be, on its scale, more effectively handled by local authorities as opposed to the Commission. Nevertheless, it would probably be accomplished more effectively by the Commission which would ensure that standards were uniform across the Community. Which test should therefore be applied the test of scale or the test of effectiveness?

Does subsidiarity already exist in Community law?

There is a view that subsidiarity has existed in Community law since its inception and that the Treaty on European Union has not introduced anything new at all.

Proportionality is a general principle of Community law which has been inspired by German law. It is a method of protecting fundamental human rights and provides that action must be proportionate to the aim that is being achieved. This acts as a break on the Community's right of action.

Another example of subsidiarity is Article 235. This provides that where where the Council lack the power to achieve a Community objective, it can acting by unanimity on a proposal from the Commission to give such power to itself.

It has also been said that Directives which leave the choice of form and methods to the Member State is an example of subsidiarity. However, the objective is fixed by the Community itself.

Preliminary references

Article 177 gives the ECJ jurisdiction to give preliminary references on questions of interpretation and validity of Community law at the request of the national court of a Member State. The procedure is for the national court to hear the case and when it encounters problems relating to the interpretation of the Treaties or the interpretation or validity of legislation the case is referred to the ECJ. After a ruling the ECJ returns the case to the national court for it to be applied to the facts of the case. So, the case starts and ends in the national courts. Article 177(2) provides that 'any court or tribunal' has a discretion to request a preliminary reference but a court against whose decision there is no judicial remedy is obliged to make a preliminary reference under Article 177(3).

Purpose of preliminary references

There are four main purposes to preliminary references.

Uniformity of interpretation

The purpose of preliminary references are to ensure uniformity of interpretation of Community law throughout the Member States. The principle of supremacy (see above) ensures that Community law prevails over national law where the two conflict. This principle would be undermined if the national courts were free to interpret Community law in their own way with the inevitable result that the law would differ from State to State. Preliminary references ensure that there is an authoritative source for interpretation. As there is a written constitution to the European Union it is possible for secondary legislation to be annulled. Preliminary references ensure that only the ECJ can give authoritative rulings on validity.

Familiarise national courts with Community legal order

They are designed to familiarise national courts with the workings of the European legal order. This has influenced the ECJ's approach to requests for references. In the early days, the ECJ was keen to encourage requests, as without them they would have been unable to develop the legal order. Consequently, the ECJ initially were not formalistic in their approach and did not make specifications about the timing or the form of the request. The ECJ also emphasised that the process involved an equal division of labour, it stressed that it was not higher in any hierarchy to the national court but was performing an equal but different role alongside the national courts. This approach was successful and the ECJ currently has a large backlog of requests, which has resulted in a shift of policy. More recently, the ECJ have become much more formalistic and it has also been argued that they are acting in more of a hierarchical manner (see below).

Develop European legal order

The ECJ has used preliminary references to develop the legal order and constitutionalise the Treaties. So it was through requests for preliminary references that the ECJ was able to develop the 'twin pillars' of direct effect (*Van Gend en Loos*) and supremacy (*Costa v ENEL*).

The ECJ has also been able to extend the scope and effectiveness of the legal order through a combination of preliminary references and Article 5. In this way it has created an interpretive obligation on Member States, to ensure that national courts interpret national legislation in accordance with the aims and purposes of directives (*Von Colson and Kamann, Marleasing);* that individuals receive compensation where they have suffered damage as a result of a Member State breaching its Community obligations (*Francovich*) and that there are effective procedural remedies to ensure the protection of Community rights (*Factortame, Emmott, Zuckerfabrik*).

Rulings on direct effect

Preliminary references have also been used to determine whether Treaty provisions and secondary legislation satisfy the criteria for direct effect and can consequently be relied upon by individuals before national courts.

What is a court or tribunal?

Article 177 only permits references from a 'court or tribunal'. Essentially the test for a 'court or tribunal' is a wide one and includes any body with official backing which exercises a judicial function, according to the normal rules of adversarial procedure.

In *Nederlandse Spoorwegen* (1973) the Dutch *Raad Van State* was held to be a court or tribunal within the meaning of Article 177. In theory, an application for judicial review in the Netherlands is decided by the Crown but based on the advice of the *Raad van State*. The ECJ took a pragmatic view and was happy to hold that the *Raad van State* was a court or tribunal within Article 177.

A commercial arbitration tribunal was held not to come within Article 177 in *Nordsee v Reederei Mond* (1982) and this rule applies even if the award of the tribunal can be enforced through the courts.

The situation is different where the arbitration body has some sort of official government backing. Consequently, in *Vaasen* (1966) a reference from a body which was an arbitration tribunal but whose members were appointed by the Dutch Minister for Social Security and operated in accordance with ordinary adversarial procedure did come within Article 177.

Similarly, in *Broekmeulen* (1981) a Dutch body called the Appeals Committee for General Medicine heard appeals from a medical disciplinary tribunal. The ability to practice as a medical practitioner was dependent on registration with the committee and one third of the Appeal Committee's members were appointed by the Dutch government. This too was held to be a 'court or tribunal' within the meaning of Article 177.

A tribunal which mixes judicial functions with other functions was still held to be a tribunal within the meaning of Article 177 in *Pretore di Salo v Persons Unknown* (1987).

In *Department of Health and Social Security (Isle of Man) v Barr and Montrose Holdings Ltd* (1991) the Deputy High Bailiff's Court in the Isle of Man was held to come within Article 177 even though only part of the provisions of Community law apply in the Isle of Man, as otherwise the uniformity of Community law would be affected.

The position is unclear as to whether international courts such as the European Court of Human Rights would be able to make a reference.

Lack of jurisdiction

Different problems arose in *Borker* (1980). The applicant was a member of the Paris Bar Council and had been refused permission to appear before a German court and applied to the Paris Bar Council. It was held that the Paris Bar Council was not a 'court or tribunal' within the meaning of Article 177 as it did not have jurisdiction to decide who appeared before a German court.

When to refer

The question of the national court's timing of a reference can only be understood in the context of the ECJ's changing policy in relation to preliminary references. In the initial stages the ECJ was keen to encourage references because without them it would have been unable to familiarise national courts with their approach and develop the legal order. Emphasis was placed on the co-operative aspects of the procedure and that there was an equal division of labour between the ECJ and the national court. As a result of this policy the ECJ was relaxed about the timing of references. Similarly, the ECJ has not been formalistic in its approach and in the past if the question has not been properly asked the ECJ re-formulates the question and asks itself the question it should have been asked.

In *R v Henn and Darby* (1981) the ECJ said that it was preferable but not essential for the facts of a case to be decided prior to a reference. The reason for its preference was that it wished to consider as many aspects of the case as possible before giving its ruling.

In the *Creamery Milk Suppliers* case (1980) the Irish High Court requested a ruling without first considering the facts. The ECJ accepted the reference and said that it was entirely for the national court's discretion as to the timing of the reference.

The ECJ became a victim of its success over the working of this co-operative policy. It has developed a backlog of cases and it takes between 18 months to two years for a preliminary reference to be heard by the ECJ. The ECJ no longer feels the need to encourage national courts to make references and in recent cases it has been prepared to take a firmer line on the timing of references.

In both *Pretore di Genova v Banchero* (1993) and *Telemarsicabruzzo SpA v Circostel* (1993) the ECJ held that the national court must define the factual and legal framework in which the questions arise before making a preliminary reference.

In both cases the ECJ said that the questions referred were so vague that they could not be answered. In both cases the ECJ emphasised its role in Article 177 proceedings which is to provide a ruling which which would be useful to a national court in the administration of justice. As both cases involved competition law the facts were particularly complicated which heightened the need for a clear description of the facts. The ECJ is trying to decrease its workload through emphasising its jurisdiction in Article 177 cases.

Discretion to refer

Under Article 177(2) *any* court or tribunal of a Member State has a discretion to make a reference to the ECJ. This right cannot be curtailed by national law (*Second Rheinmühlen* case (1974)) and it cannot be fettered by a regulation of the Communities (*BRT-Sabam* case (1974)).

The principles under which a British court should exercise its discretion were originally indicated by Lord Denning MR in *Bulmer v Bollinger* (1974) when he said that the decision must be necessary to enable the English court to give judgment. In deciding whether the reference is necessary account must be taken of the following factors:

- the decision of the question must be conclusive of the case;
- is there a previous ruling by the ECJ of the issue?
- is the provision *acte clair*?
- the facts of the case must have been decided.

If the court decides that a decision is necessary it must still consider the following factors:

- delay;
- the difficulty and importance of the point;
- expense;
- burden on the ECJ;

- wishes of the parties;
- difficulty in framing the question in sufficiently clear terms to benefit from a ruling.

These criteria have been attacked on the grounds that they are unduly restrictive and delaying because of the expense and burden on the parties may, in fact, increase their expenses if a referral has to be made by a higher court.

More recently, the correct approach has been redefined by Sir Thomas Bingham MR in *R v International Stock Exchange of the United Kingdom and the Republic of Ireland ex p Else* (1993). In his view three points needed to be considered in deciding whether to make a referral:

- firstly, find the facts;
- secondly, is the Community law provision critical to the outcome?
- thirdly, can the court resolve the provision of Community law with complete confidence?

In addition, the court must be mindful of four factors when making its decision:

- national courts must be fully mindful of the differences between national law and Community law;
- pitfalls of entering into an unfamiliar field;
- need for uniform interpretation;
- advantage enjoyed by ECJ in interpreting Community legislation.

Bingham MR's formulation is weighted more heavily in favour of a referral than Lord Denning's. Walsh 56 (1993) MLR 881 feels that there will be more successful appeals against the decision to refer under Bingham's formulation than existed previously. He argues that Lord Denning's approach is more subjective and that higher courts are loath to overrule a subjective decision. As Bingham's formulation is much more objective it will be easier for a higher court to overrule a decision to refer.

Obligation to refer

Article 177(3) provides that a court or tribunal against whose decision there is no judicial remedy is obliged to make a reference to the ECJ. There are two differing views as to what is meant by the phrase 'a court or tribunal against whose decision there is no judicial remedy'.

- 'Abstract theory'– that it can only mean the highest court in the land. In the UK it would be the House of Lords. This view was supported by Lord Denning in *Bulmer v Bollinger*.

- 'Concrete theory' – courts which are judging in final instance in that particular case. For example, to appeal from the Court of Appeal to the House of Lords it is necessary to have leave. If leave is not forthcoming then the Court of Appeal is the highest court in that particular case. There is *obiter dicta* supporting this theory in *Costa v ENEL* (1964). In *Hagen* (1980) the Court of Appeal held that it is bound to make a reference under Article 177 if leave to appeal to the House of Lords is not obtainable.
- In theory, the Commission can bring enforcement proceedings against a Member State whose highest court does not make a preliminary reference but in practice the Commission does not do so.
- *Acte Clair* – the ECJ has sanctioned the use of *acte clair* from French law, subject to conditions, where the question is clear and free from doubt. If an act is *acte clair* even a court that comes within Article 177(3) is freed from its obligation to refer.

In *CILFIT v Italian Minister of Health* (1982) the doctrine of *acte clair* was accepted by the ECJ, when it said that an application would not be 'necessary' if:

- the question of Community law was irrelevant;
- the provision had already been interpreted by the ECJ;
- the correct application is so obvious it leaves no room for doubt.

In addition to these criteria the national court must also be convinced that the answer would be equally obvious to a court in another Member State, as well as the ECJ. The national court must compare the different versions of the text in the various Community languages. It must also bear in mind that legal concepts and terminology do not necessarily have the same meaning in Community law as national law.

These last criteria deprive the doctrine of *acte clair* of much of its practical effect. The national judge must be satisfied that not only is the provision free from doubt in his own language but he must peruse the text in the other nine languages and taking into account the different legal concepts in the different jurisdictions must be still be satisfied that the matter is free from doubt; an immense challenge even for the most accomplished linguist. The narrowness with which the doctrine has been drawn is a reflection of the advantage the ECJ has over national courts in interpreting legislation and comparing the different texts.

Validity

It was held in *Foto-Frost v Hauptzollamt Lübeck-Ost* (1987) by the ECJ that national courts could not find Community legislation invalid. So the *acte clair* doctrine cannot apply to questions of invalidity but it is possible for national courts to find Community acts valid. An exception exists in cases of interlocutory proceedings where national courts for reasons of urgency can rule that Community acts are invalid on an interim basis. In *Zuckerfabrik Süderditmarschen v Hauptzollmat Itzehoe* (1991) it was held a Community act could be declared temporarily invalid, provided:

- it has serious doubts about the validity of the Community act;
- it asks the ECJ for a preliminary ruling on the validity of the act;
- the matter is urgent and the applicant will suffer serious and irreparable damage if relief is refused; and
- due account is taken of the interest of the Community and the need to ensure the effectiveness of Community law.

The ECJ will not overrule a provision of national law in a preliminary reference but it can say that a rule of national law is inapplicable in a Community context by providing guidance on the correct interpretation of Community law.

Can the ECJ refuse to hear a reference?

In recent years this has been one of the most vexed questions in relation to preliminary references and a popular topic with examiners.

The ECJ will decline to hear a reference where it falls outside of Article 177. If the reference is not made by a court or tribunal as in *Borker* and *Nordsee* then it will decline to hear a case.

If the reference is nothing to do with Community law then the ECJ will decline the reference (*Alderblum*). The fact that the reference has nothing to do with Community law does not mean that it will have been without merit. The national judge will be free to apply national law safe in the knowledge that Community law is not relevant.

Absence of Genuine Dispute

In *Foglia v Novello (No 1)* (1980) the questions referred concerned an import tax imposed by the French on the import of wine from Italy. The litigation was between two Italian parties. Foglia was a wine producer and agreed to sell wine to Novello, who was an exporter. In order to challenge the French tax a clause was inserted into the contract that Foglia would not have to be pay any duties levied by the French authorities which was in contravention of Community law. The parties were agreed that the tax was illegal and the contractual clause was a device to ensure that the matter could be brought before a court.

The ECJ refused to hear a reference from the Italian court. The ECJ felt that an Italian court was attempting to challenge a French tax and this was abusing the preliminary reference procedure, as it was an indirect method of bringing enforcement proceedings. The ECJ declined to hear the reference on the grounds that there was an absence of a genuine dispute between the parties. The case was returned to the Italian court and the judge re-formulated the questions and referred the matter again to the ECJ. The ECJ again refused to hear the case in *Foglia v Novello (No 2)* (1981).

The case has been criticised on the grounds that the ECJ had entered into a review of the national court's decision to refer. The purpose of Article 177 is that there should be co-operation between national courts and the ECJ. If the ECJ is to enter into inquiries as to whether the national court's decision to refer is a correct decision then it is exercising some sort of appellate jurisdiction. The ECJ had always been keen to emphasise that it performed an equal but different role in relation to Article 177 proceedings but in the *Foglia* cases it suggested that it was, by reviewing decisions of national courts, higher in a hierarchy to national courts.

The approach adopted in the *Foglia* cases has not really been followed in later cases.

Hypothetical Questions

In *Mattheus v Doego* (1978) the ECJ refused to hear hypothetical questions relating to the effect accession to the Community would have on contractual relations of private parties on the basis that the ECJ cannot determine in advance the outcome of negotiations or of the political act resulting in the admission of a State to the Community.

This was followed in *Meilicke v ADV/ORGA FA Meyer AG* (1992) when again the ECJ refused to hear hypothetical questions. In *Meilicke* a German lawyer had written books and articles in learned journals against the theory of disguised non-cash subscriptions of capital which he submitted was contrary to the Second Company Directive. He held a single share in a company which decided to increase capital by 5 million DM. At an Annual General Meeting of the company, he tried to find out if the money was used to reduce the company's debts to the bank which was the guarantor of the newly issued shares. The answers to those questions would determine whether or not the capital amounted to a disguised non-cash subscription. The directors declined to give him the information.

Both Meilicke and the company were agreed that contributions in kind would be incompatible with the Directive. There was no real dispute and the proceedings had been contrived so as to ensure that the ECJ answered the questions. The ECJ refused to give a ruling on the basis that they were hypothetical questions and were beyond the jurisdiction of the ECJ as the answers were not needed for the administration of justice. The approach differs from that taken in the *Foglia* cases as the ECJ is no longer prepared to look at the national court's reasons for making a reference but instead emphasise the jurisdiction they have been given under Article 177 and the need for national courts to respect their role.

Effect of a preliminary reference

A preliminary reference is binding on the national court which referred the question for consideration.

They may also be cited as precedents in common law jurisdictions (*WH Smith Do It All and Payless DIY Ltd v Peterborough City Council* (1990)).

Revision Notes

Direct effect

Criteria for direct effect

Before any type of legislation can have direct effect whether it be a treaty provision, regulation, directive or decision it must satisfy the criteria for direct effect.

These can be summarised as follows:

- clear and unambiguous;
- unconditional;
- not dependent on further action (*Reyners v Belgium*).

Direct effect of Treaty provisions

It was held in *Van Gend en Loos* (1963) that Treaty provisions (which satisfy the criteria) have vertical direct effect ie they impose obligations on national governments and create corresponding rights for citizens.

This was held to extend to positive obligations in *Alfons Lütticke GmbH v Commission* (1966).

It was held in *Defrenne (No 2)* (1976) that Treaty provisions (which satisfy the criteria) have horizontal direct effect ie they impose obligations as well as create rights for citizens.

Direct effect of regulations

Article 189 provides that regulations are directly applicable ie they apply in the Member States without the need for national implementing legislation.

Regulations which satisfy the criteria also have direct effect. Regulations are capable of both horizontal and vertical direct effect.

Direct effect of directives

The Treaty is silent on the question of the direct effect of Directives.

The Court of Justice held that a provision of a Directive which specified the commencement date of a Treaty provision had direct effect in *Franz Grad v Finanzamt Traunstein* (1970) and a substantive provision of a Directive was held to have direct effect in *Van Duyn v Home Office* (1974).

The Court of Justice's main reasons for giving direct effect to Directives is to make them more effective and to estop Member States from relying on their own wrongdoing.

There are two main limitations on the direct effect of Directives:

- they do not have direct effect before their time limit has expired (*Ratti* (1979));
- they do not have horizontal direct effect (*Marshall (No 1)* (1986)).

A Directive still has direct effect even though it has been transposed into national law (*VNO v Inspecteur der Invoerrechten en Accijnzen* (1977)).

Direct effect of decisions

It was held in *Franz Grad* (1970) that decisions have direct effect (provided they satisfy the criteria).

International agreements

Agreements with non-Member States are directly effective (*Kupferberg* (1982)) provided they satisfy the criteria.

Limitations on doctrine of direct effect

There are three main limitations on the doctrine of direct effect:

- not all provisions satisfy the criteria;
- Directives do not have direct effect until their time limit has expired;
- Directives do not have horizontal direct effect.

In more recent times there are two main ways in which these problems have been circumvented; through the interpretive obligation and the creation of a right of damages against national governments.

Interpretive obligation (indirect effect)

This helps to some extent to circumvent the problem of the lack of horizontal direct effect of Directives, their lack of direct effect until their time limit has expired and the need to satisfy the criteria for direct effect.

In *Von Colson* (1984) it was held that national legislation must be interpreted by national courts in accordance with the aims and purposes of a directive, including provisions of a Directive which lack direct effectiveness, 'in so far as is possible'.

In *Kolpinghuis Nijmegen* (1987) it was held that national legislation must be interpreted in accordance with a Directive *before* the time limit for its implementation has expired provided that this does not infringe the principles of legal certainty and non-retroactivity.

In *Marleasing* (1992) it was held that national courts must interpret national legislation as being in accordance with a Directive even if this leads to an individual being able to rely on a Directive as against another individual. Again the obligation was limited to 'so far as it is possible'.

The basis for the interpretive obligation is Article 5.

Although the interpretive obligation has successfully given individuals rights in situations where Directives lack direct effect, before time limits have expired and where an individual wishes to rely on a directive as against another individual, it is limited by this qualification 'as far as possible'. Maltby argues that this means that the obligation only arises where there are genuinely two ways in which to interpret national legislation.

Remedies against national governments

The case of *Francovich* (1992) held that on the basis of Article 5, Member States must compensate individuals who have suffered loss as a result of their breach of Community obligations. Three conditions must be satisfied:

- the Directive must confer rights on individuals;
- the content of the rights must be identifiable;
- there must be a causal link between the breach and damage suffered.

In *Francovich* the applicant obtained compensation where the applicant suffered loss as a result of a failure to implement a non-directly effective provision.

In *Marshall (No 2)* (1993) damages were awarded for the incorrect transposition of a directly effective provision of a Directive. Compensation must be awarded in full for the loss and the value of the award must be protected by the payment of interest.

The right of action in damages ensures that where an individual has suffered loss as a result of one of the limitations on direct effect then they can be compensated by an action for damages against the State.

Procedural remedies

In addition to substantive rights to damages the ECJ has also created procedural remedies.

Where there is a rule of national law preventing the grant of interim relief to protect a Community right then a national court must set aside that rule (*Factortame (No 1)* (1990)).

Where a directive has been incorrectly transposed then time does not start to run for limitation periods until the directive has been correctly transposed (*Emmott v Minister for Social Welfare* (1991)).

Administrative acts based on a Community measure can only be suspended on the same basis as the conditions applied by the ECJ (*Zuckerfabrik* (1991)).

Primacy

Community law takes priority over conflicting provisions of national law, regardless of whether the national law is earlier or later in time (*Costa v ENEL* (1964)).

Community law overrules conflicting provisions of national constitutions (*Internationale Handelsgesellschaft* (1970)).

The national court must apply the principle of supremacy immediately (*Simmenthal* (1978)).

Member States cannot argue that they are unable to apply the principle of supremacy due to *force majeure* (*Art Treasures cases* (1968) and (1970)).

The principle of supremacy applies regardless of whether the conflicting provision of national law is criminal or civil in character (*Dassonville* (1974)).

Member States are under an obligation to repeal conflicting provisions of national law (*French Merchant Seamen* case (1974)).

Subsidiarity

This is a principle first introduced into the environment provisions of the Single European Act and made a general principle under the Treaty on European Union.

Article 3(b) provides that in matters which do not fall within exclusive Community competence, action will only be taken by the Community if the action cannot be sufficiently achieved by the Member States and because of the scale of the proposed action is more effectively achieved by the Community.

It is doubtful whether subsidiarity is a legal principle at all and it is felt to contain an inherent contradiction.

Preliminary references

Article 177
The European Court has jurisdiction to give preliminary rulings concerning:

(a) the interpretation of the Treaty;
(b) the validity and interpretation of acts of Community institutions and of the ECB;
(c) the interpretation of statutes of bodies established by Council.

Any court or tribunal of a member State may, if it considers that a decision thereon is necessary to enable it to give judgment, request the court to give a ruling.

A court or tribunal of a member State against whose decision there is no judicial remedy under national law shall bring the matter before the European Court.

Purpose of a preliminary reference:

* to ensure uniformity of interpretation;
* familiarises national courts with the application of the Community legal order and helps them overcome difficulties in applying this legal order;
* helps develop the Community legal order – *Van Gend en Loos, Costa v ENEL;*
* to decide whether a Community act has direct effect.

What is a court or tribunal?

* *Nederlandse Spoorwegen* (1973), the Dutch *Raad von State;*
* *Vaasen* (1966);
* *Broekmeulen* (1981);
* *Borker* (1980).

When to refer?

* *R v Henn* (1981);
* *Irish Creamery Milk Suppliers Association v Ireland* (1981).

Discretion to refer Article 177(2):

* right cannot be curtailed by national law (*Second Rheinmühlen* case (1974));
* cannot be fettered by a regulation of the Communities (*BRT v Sabam* (1974));

- principles on which a British court has exercised its discretion (*HP Bulmer and Sons Ltd v JA Bollinger SA* (1974) *per* Lord Denning).

First, the court should consider whether the reference is necessary taking into account the following factors:

- does the outcome of the case depend on the correct interpretation of Community law?
- is there any previous ruling by the ECJ on the issue?
- is the provision *acte clair*?
- the facts of the case should be decided first.

Secondly, having decided that the reference is necessary the national court should then consider whether to exercise its discretion by taking into account the following factors:

- inconvenience caused by the delay;
- need to avoid overloading the ECJ;
- difficulty in framing the question in sufficiently clear terms to benefit from a ruling;
- difficulty and importance of the provision in question;
- expense;
- the wishes of the parties.

Lord Denning's guidelines were applied in *Customs and Excise Commissioners v ApS Samex Ltd* (1983).

More recently the correct approach has been redefined in *R v International Stock Exchange of the United Kingdom and the Republic of Ireland ex p Else and ors* (1993) *per* Sir Thomas Bingham MR.

Three points need to be considered in deciding whether to make a referral:

- firstly, find the facts;
- secondly, is the Community law provision critical to the outcome?
- thirdly, can the court resolve the provision of Community law with complete confidence?

In addition the court must be mindful of four factors when making its decision:

- national court must be fully mindful of the differences between national law and Community law;
- pitfalls of entering into an unfamiliar field;
- need for uniform interpretation;
- advantage enjoyed by ECJ in interpreting Community legislation.

Obligation to refer Article 177(3):

- Abstract theory – *Bulmer v Bollinger;*
- Concrete theory – *Costa v ENEL* (1964) *Hagen v Moretti* (1980);
- Article 169.

Acte Clair

CILFIT v Italian Minister of Health (1982)

- the question of whether EC law is irrelevant;
- the provision has already been interpreted by the ECJ;
- the correct application is so obvious it leaves no room for doubt.

  The following factors should also be taken into account:

- the national court must be convinced that the answer would be equally obvious to a court in another Member State;
- the national court must compare the different versions of the text in the different Community languages;
- it must also be borne in mind that legal concepts and terminology do not necessarily have the same meaning in Community law as national law.

Should the ECJ ever refuse a request for a preliminary reference?

- where the issue referred has nothing to do with Community law: *Alderblum;*
- where the requirements of Article 177 are not satisfied *(Borker);*
- where the reference is an abuse of procedure *(Mattheus* (1978));
- *Foglia v Novello* (1980);
- *Foglia v Novello* (No 2) (1981);
- fictitious litigation?

Effect of a preliminary ruling:

- a preliminary ruling is binding on the national court hearing the case for which the decision is given *(First Milch-, Fett und Eier* case (1969));
- In common law jurisdictions they are binding precedents *(WH Smith Do-It-All and Payless DIY Ltd v Peterborough City Council* (1990)).

3 Community institutions

You should be familiar with the following areas: ✓

- European Parliament
- Commission
- Council of the European Union
- European Council
- Court of Justice
- Court of First Instance
- Court of Auditors
- Economic and Social Committee, Committee of Regions, COREPER, European Investment Bank

The Commission

Functions

Initiator of community action

The Commission has historically had the right of legislative initiative and Council decisions are taken on the basis of Commission proposals. The Treaty on European Union allows the European Parliament by an overall majority to 'request' that the Commission submits proposals. To a certain extent, this is a dilution of the Commission's right of initiative.

The Commission shares the right of legislative initiative in respect of the two other pillars of the European Union introduced by the Treaty on European Union. In common foreign and security policy matters the right to submit proposals is shared with Member States. In judicial and home affairs matters, Member States have the right of initiative on all matters, while the Commission have the right of initiative in respect of some matters.

'Watchdog'

The Commission acts as the 'watchdog' of the European Community ensuring that the law is enforced either through enforcement proceedings or through its role in competition law.

Articles 169-170

The Commission is in a unique position regarding enforcement proceedings. Under Article 169 proceedings the Commission can take Member States which are in breach of their Treaty obligations before the ECJ. The procedure is in two stages. The first is an informal stage whereby the Commission issues a formal notice and eventually issues a reasoned opinion to the Member State which delimits the nature of the dispute. In practice, the Commission attempts to negotiate a settlement with the Member State and in 1990 approximately 78% of cases were settled at an informal stage. The second stage is the formal, litigation stage where the Commission takes the errant Member State before the ECJ.

Article 170 proceedings involve one Member State taking another before the ECJ but even with this procedure the Member State must first take its complaint before the Commission which will issue a reasoned opinion. In practice, if there is substance to the complaint then the Commission will take the complaint over and consequently Article 170 is rarely used.

As the Commission is involved in all enforcement proceedings and negotiates the outcome of the majority of such proceedings it is in a distinctive position. Snyder 56 (1993) MLR 19 argues that this enables the Commission to use litigation to develop long term strategies and establish basic principles. For example, in the years prior to the 1 January 1993 deadline for the European Internal Market, most enforcement proceedings related to the non-implementation of Directives. Article 169 was being used as a tool to ensure the success of the Internal Market programme.

Competition law

The Commission is also the watchdog for the Community's competition law policy. Under regulation 17/62 it has the power to impose fines and penalties on individuals for the breach of Articles 85 and 86. It is also the only body empowered to grant exemptions for restrictive agreements under Article 85. These can take one of two forms; an individual or block exemption. As the Commission is the only body empowered to grant exemption then its unique position enables it to formulate its own policies in respect of them. Whish argues that block exemptions become a 'model' agreement and therefore imposes conditions on the parties which they would not agree to if they had been allowed to freely negotiate contracts. Also, it can be seen that the nature of individual exemptions has changed in response to changing economic circumstances. Initially, it favoured granting exemption to agreements made between small and medium sized enterprises. More recently, in response to an increasing threat from American and Japanese competition, it has been more prepared to grant exemption to large enterprises to enable them to compete more effectively on a global scale.

Executive of the Community

The Commission is often called the executive of the Community. The term is misleading and the Commission's role has fluctuated between a prototype federal government and a secretariat simply carrying out the instructions of the Council of the European Union. The change in role has been a response to historical circumstances. Unlike the Parliament which has seen a steady increase in its powers since the Treaty of Rome; the Commission has seen peaks and troughs in its powers. The key dates are as follows:

1958-1965

This was the highpoint of the Commission's powers when it seemed to be evolving into some sort of federal government. It negotiated the elimination of customs tariffs and a common agricultural policy, although it had less success with the establishment of a common external tariff, internal liberalising measures and energy and transport policy.

1966

In response to a constitutional crises in the Community the Luxembourg compromise was developed. Where the vital interests of a Member State are at stake it can veto a legislative proposal. The Community was put on a more intergovernmentalist footing and the Commission took on more of the characteristics of a secretariat.

1974

This year saw the formation of the European Council. This again gave a more intergovernmentalist flavour to the Community.

1986

The 1993 deadline for the European Internal Market, enhanced the Commission's role. It became more active in the legislative sphere and in negotiation with national governments. The European Internal Market programme was largely completed on schedule.

1993

This year saw the coming into force of the Treaty on European Union. The Commission was on the wane again and the right of the legislative initiative diluted. The new 1993 legislative procedure in Article 189b only allows for the Commission to mediate in the Conciliation Committee and its proposals can be amended by a qualified majority. This weakens the Commission as it makes its proposals easier to change.

The Commission has a small primary legislative power. In *France, Italy and United Kingdom v Commission* (1980) it was held that the Commission had a right to legislate where it is clear from a purposive interpretation of a Treaty provision that it was intended to give such a right to the Commission.

The Commission is often involved in the detailed implementation of Council decisions. This frequently involves further legislation and as a result the Commission has been given wide powers of delegated legislation. The Council has not relinquished total control over the delegated legislation and retains varying degrees of control through the committees system.

Recommendations and opinions

The Commission can formulate recommendations or opinions on matters dealt with in the Treaty.

Representative, financial and administrative functions

The Commission has a number of representative, financial and administrative functions. It represents the Member States in negotiations with non-Member States. It is responsible for the administration of Community funds.

It administers four special funds:

* European Social Fund;
* Cohesion Fund;
* European Agricultural Guidance and Guarantee Fund;
* European Regional Development Fund.

Composition

There are 17 members of the Commission who are appointed by the governments of the Member States. They must all be nationals of the Member States and no more than two can be nationals of the same

State. In practice, each of the five larger States: France, Italy, Germany, Spain and the United Kingdom have two Commissioners and the smaller States have one.

Under Article 11 Merger Treaty the Commissioners must be appointed by 'common accord'. Each appointment must be agreed to by all the Member States and since the Treaty on European Union the Parliament can veto the appointment of Commissioners.

Despite the careful attention to the representation of each Member State, Commissioners are not the representatives of national governments and are required to act in the interests of the Union, as a whole. They are required to be above national loyalties.

The Commission act as a college and they must all be agreed on a proposal before it is sent to the Council. It is headed by a President and there can be one or two Vice-Presidents.

There are 23 departments known as Directorates General. Each Directorate General is headed by a Director General, who is responsible to the relevant Commissioner. Directorates General are sub-divided into Directorates (headed by a Director) and these in turn are made up of Divisions (each under a Head of Division).

Each Commissioner is assisted by his *Cabinet*, which is a type of private office and consists of a group of officials appointed by him and directly responsible to him. The head of the *Cabinet* is known as the *Chef de Cabinet*. The *Chefs de Cabinet* meet regularly to co-ordinate activities and prepare the ground for Commission meetings. If the *Chefs de Cabinet* reach unanimous agreement on a question then their decision is normally adopted by the Commission without debate.

Commissioners are appointed for four year renewable terms. All the terms expire together so the whole of the Commission is reappointed at the same time. National governments cannot dismiss the Commission during a term of office; they can only fail to renew a term.

The Commission can be forced to resign *en bloc* by the Parliament but this cannot be used to dismiss individual Commissioners.

The ECJ can compel a Commissioner to retire on the ground of serious misconduct or because he no longer fulfils the conditions required for the performance of his duties.

Council of the European Union

The purpose of the Council of European Union is to represent the interests of the Member States.

Functions
Its functions are:

- to take general policy decisions;
- to ensure objectives set out in Treaty are attained (Article 145);
- to ensure co-ordination of general economic policies of Member States (Article 145);
- the power to take decisions (generally based on Commission proposals);
- to conclude agreements with foreign countries;
- to jointly decide budget with Parliament;
- Article 235 enables the Council to legislate on the basis of a Commission proposal and after consulting the Parliament, in order to achieve a Treaty objective but where it lacks the specific power.

Composition
The Council is not a fixed body, each Member State is represented by a government minister. The government minister who attends the meeting will depend on the subject matter of the meeting. When general matters are discussed the Member States are represented by their foreign ministers and it will be called a 'general council'. In addition, there are 'specialised' or 'technical' councils where the Member States will be represented by the government minister responsible for that particular specialisation. The Council is assisted by a General Secretariat, which is headed by a Secretary General.

Presidency
The Presidency of the Council rotates amongst the members at six monthly intervals. While it holds the Presidency, a Member State will provide a President (chairman) for all meetings of the Council. The President will call meetings, preside at them, call for a vote and sign acts adopted at the meeting. The Presidency also has responsibility to ensure the smooth running of the Council and will act as mediator between the Member States when searching for an agreement and is the Union's representative to the outside world.

To a large extent the Presidency will enable a Member State to control the agenda of the European Union, so a Member State will attempt to use the time that it holds the Presidency to push through as many measures as possible.

COREPER

The government ministers who comprise the Council of the European Union will have full time ministerial responsibilities in their own country and as a result are only present in Brussels for short periods.

In order to provide continuity a Committee of Permanent Representatives, known as COREPER was established.

Each Member State has an ambassador to the Union and these ambassadors are given the title Permanent Representatives and their function is to represent the Member States at a lower level than the ministers.

Article 151(1) charges COREPER with responsibility for preparing work of the Council and carrying out the tasks assigned to it by Council.

In fact, there are two tiers to COREPER itself. Important political questions are dealt with by the Permanent Representatives themselves, this is known as COREPER 11.

More technical questions will be dealt with by deputy Permanent Representatives meeting known as COREPER 1.

At a lower level still COREPER is involved in the work of a plethora of sub-committees and working groups which examine Commission proposals. In these meetings the Member State is often represented by a national expert.

COREPER has been called a 'mixed' institution which is in this 'grey zone' of institutions that cannot be classified as belonging either to the Union or to Member States.

Hayes-Renshaw, Lequesne and Mayor Lopez 28 (1989) JCMS 119 discovered that while the Permanent Representatives carry out the instructions of their national capitals, they also develop a loyalty to each other as a group built up over a course of dealing consisting of many hours of meetings. Their desire to defend national interests is matched by a desire to reach agreement, they perceive a necessity to engage in 'log-rolling': trading compromises on one issue in return for concessions on another unrelated matter, in order to reach agreement.

They also see their role as educating their national governments as to the nature of the decision making process and acting as a bridge between experts from the Commission and Member States on one hand and Commissioners and national governments on the other.

Voting

Article 148(1) provides: 'Save as otherwise provided in this Treaty, the Council shall act by a majority of its members.'

In practice, only a few unimportant matters are decided by a simple majority. Some matters eg admission of new members are decided unanimously. Most matters are decided by a 'qualified majority' with the votes of larger States have greater weight than the votes of smaller States. Under Article 148(2) the votes of the Member States are weighted, as follows:

Country	Votes
Germany, France, Italy, UK	10 votes
Spain	8 votes
Belgium, Greece, Netherlands, Portugal	5 votes
Denmark, Ireland	3 votes
Luxembourg	2 votes
	76 total

A qualified majority is 54 votes. Although bigger States have a bigger vote than smaller States, the latter still have more votes than they would be entitled to on a *per capita* basis and the figure of 54 votes means that the larger States cannot outvote the smaller States.

Luxembourg Accords

In addition to the above rules there is a constitutional convention known as the 'Luxembourg Accords' which requires that discussions be continued until unanimity is achieved before a decision can be taken which affects the vital national interests of a Member State.

This does not have the force of law but has been followed in practice. The veto will not be allowed where its use is 'improper'. In May 1982 the UK attempted to invoke the veto to prevent an increase in the price of agricultural products. It was conceded by the UK that the issue did not involve vital national interests but they were attempting to force concessions on another issue. This was not accepted by the other Member States as a proper use of the veto and the proposals were adopted. This incident was a watershed and marked the beginning of the decline of the Luxembourg Accords. It was no longer left to the Member State to define what its vital national interests were.

The Single European Act seems to have put an end to the Luxembourg Accords. Despite the British Foreign Secretary telling the House of Commons in 1986 and 1990 that they were unaffected by the Single European Act the only attempt to use the veto since the Act came into force by Greece in 1988 was unsuccessful. This has led Teasdale 31 (1993) JCMS 567 to declare that, '... the Luxembourg Compromise effectively died with the Single European Act'.

Tactics have essentially changed in relation to legislation that Member States do not like. The UK's current tactic is to challenge the legal basis of disputed legislation rather than seek to impose a veto.

European Council

In 1974 it was agreed that the Heads of State or of government of the Member States, together with their foreign ministers, would hold summit conferences at regular intervals. These became known as the 'European Council' and achieved legal status by virtue of Article 2 of the Single European Act. The President of the Commission has also been given the right to attend meetings.

The title 'European Council' is confusing as it is different to the Council of Ministers, although it can act as a Council of Ministers, as there is nothing to prevent Member States being represented by their Heads of State or government.

The European Council possesses no formal powers. It is a forum for discussions, on an informal basis, relating to issues of common Community concern and it is a vehicle for co-ordination of the Member States' foreign policies to ensure that they maximise their influence on world affairs. To this end the Single European Act places an obligation, 'to endeavour jointly to formulate and implement a European foreign policy'.

Article D of the Treaty on European Union provides a further role for the European Council when it states that it shall:

...provide the Union with the necessary impetus for its development and shall define the general political guidelines thereof.

The European Council is the focus of the intergovernmentalist activities under the common foreign and security and economic and monetary union pillars of the European Union.

The Presidency of the European Council is held by the Member State that holds the Presidency of the Council of Ministers.

European Parliament

The purpose of the European Parliament is to represent the peoples of the Member States.

Seats (each) (following 1994 direct elections):

Germany	99
France, UK and Italy	87
Spain	64
Netherlands	31
Belgium, Greece, Portugal	25
Denmark	16
Ireland	15
Luxembourg	6
	567

European political groups

European political party groups as opposed to national groups exist in the European Parliament. There are rules for the determination of recognition of European political groups. There must be 23 MEPs to form a political group if they all come from one Member State; at least 18 if they come from two Member States and 12 if they come from three. The purpose of emphasising European groupings is to assist the process of European integration and to encourage political thinking to develop along pan-European lines.

Qualification of a member of European Parliament

Although an MEP can be a member of the national parliament, MEPs are not allowed to be members of the government of a Member State, member of the Commission, Court of Justice, Court of Auditors, Economic and Social Committee, Consultative Committee of the ECSC, active official or servant of any of the Community institutions or specialised body attached to them, or Registrar of the Court.

Powers and duties

The powers of the European Parliament can be categorised as follows:

- supervisory function;
- participation in legislative process;
- budgetary;
- special powers.

Supervisory function

The Commission is politically accountable to the Parliament. The Parliament consequently has a number of powers to hold the Commission accountable:

- the Commission has to reply orally or in writing to questions put to it by the Parliament (Article 140);
- can demand resignation of Commission *en bloc*;
- debates the annual report produced by the Commission;
- system of Parliamentary Committees which prepare decisions of the Parliament and maintains regular contact with the Commission when the Parliament is not sitting.

Members of the Commission participate in Parliamentary debates and Parliament uses its budgetary powers to hold the Commission accountable.

It has been argued that the supervisory powers over the Commission are too powerful to be used. Although it can demand the resignation of the Commission *en bloc*, the old Commission would continue until a new Commission was appointed by the governments of the Member States and the Parliament would have no say in the appointment of a new Commission. The Treaty on European Union rectifies this by giving the Parliament a power of veto over the appointment of Commissioners, so the Parliament's hand has been strengthened in relation to this power. The problem is that the Parliament does not usually have an argument with the Commission as the two institutions are natural allies, both seeing things from a Community perspective while the Council which represents the interests of the Member States has a more nationalistic approach.

The Parliament also exercises supervisory powers over the Council. Although not obliged to do so, the Council replies to written questions and through the President of the relevant Council formation, to oral questions. Council Presidents are invited to appear before Parliamentary committees and attend plenary sessions to give the views of Council or give an account of Council business. A problem in supervising the Council arises from the fact that it represents the national interest and therefore speaks with a discordant voice.

The Treaty on European Union has given additional supervisory powers to the Parliament:

- Parliament will have the right to set up temporary Committees of Inquiry to investigate 'alleged contraventions or maladministration in the implementation of Community law' (except where the matter is *sub judice*);
- any citizen of the Union or any resident of a Member State has the right to petition the European Parliament on a matter within Community competence which affects him directly;

• the Parliament is to appoint an Ombudsman who will be empowered to receive complaints concerning instances of maladministration in the activities of Community institutions or bodies (except the Court of Justice and the Court of First Instance).

Participation in the legislative process

There are four different legislative processes: consultation procedure, co-operation procedure, co-decision procedure and assent. The relevant procedure and consequently the Parliament's involvement in the process is governed by the Treaties.

Consultative function

One of the Parliament's main functions has traditionally been to advise and be consulted on proposed legislation. Prior to the Single European Act the Treaties only gave the European Parliament a right to be consulted in the legislative process. The consultation procedure still exists in relation to the Common Agricultural Policy, provisions relating to aspects of environmental policy, harmonisation of indirect taxation, visa policy and several articles relating to Economic and Monetary Union.

The Commission forwards a proposal to the Council, which in turn forwards it to the Parliament for its opinion. The proposal is passed to the appropriate Parliamentary Committee before a plenary session of Parliament gives its opinion. There is no obligation on the Commission or the Council to follow this opinion. However, failure to consult the Parliament where there is a Treaty requirement so to do is a breach of an 'essential procedural requirement' and the legislation will be annulled (*Roquette v Council* (1980); *Maizena v Council* (1980)).

There is no requirement on the Commission to consult the Parliament while formulating a proposal. However, the Parliament can use its supervisory power over the Commission to indirectly influence the Council in the consultation procedure. The Council takes its decisions on the basis of Commission proposals. The Commission would want its proposals to enjoy broad support from the Parliament as the former is accountable to the latter. In this indirect way the Parliament can bring pressure to bear to ensure that its opinions are respected. The Parliament's power over Commission proposals has been strengthened by the Treaty on European Union, which provides that the Parliament can 'request' proposals from the Commission. If the Council substantially amends a proposal after receiving the Parliament's opinion then there is an obligation to consult the Parliament again (*European Parliament v Council* (1992)).

Co-operation procedure

The Single European Act introduced a new legislative procedure which gave the Parliament greater say over legislation. This involves two readings on the part of the Council and the Parliament. Initially the co-operation procedure was used for legislative measures for completion of the internal market.

The Treaty on European Union has brought a significant change to the co-operation procedure and for most of the decisions for which the co-operation procedure was required the procedure referred to in Article 189b is now used. New uses have been created for the co-operation procedure and it is now used in connection with the common transport policy, vocational training, environment and common development co-operation.

The procedure works by following initially the same process as the the consultation procedure but the Council will adopt a 'common position' at the end of this first reading.

The Parliament can approve the 'common position' or do nothing for three months, in which case the 'common position' will be adopted.

The second option is for the Parliament to reject the 'common position' by an absolute majority of its members; however, the Council can still adopt the legislation but only if it acts unanimously.

The third option is for the Parliament to propose amendments to the 'common position' by an absolute majority of its members. The Commission must then re-examine the proposal and either adopt the Parliament's proposals or leave its own original proposal intact. The re-examined proposal is sent back to the Council which can adopt it by a qualified majority or amend it unanimously.

Although the co-operation procedure does not give a power of veto to the Parliament, it forces the Council to take account of its views more directly than the consultation procedure.

Procedure referred to in Article 189b

Technically, it is incorrect to call this procedure 'co-decision', as it does not give the Parliament equal rights of approval over the legislative procedure. Nevertheless, the Parliament's influence over legislation has been increased still further where the procedure has been used. The correct term is the 'procedure referred to in Article 189b'.

The procedure is for the Commission to send its proposals to both the Council and the Parliament. Apart from this, the procedure for the first reading is the same as for the co-operation procedure. The Council will adopt a 'common position' which can be approved, rejected or amended by the Parliament.

If the Parliament approves or fails to signify its intentions then the measure is adopted.

If the Parliament rejects the 'common position' then the Council may convene the Conciliation Committee, which consists of equal members of the Council and Commission, with the Commission acting as an honest broker. If the Parliament still rejects the 'common position' then the measure is effectively vetoed and will lapse.

Where the Parliament proposes amendments, the amended text is sent to both the Council and the Commission. The Council can accept and adopt this amended proposal, or if it is not accepted, the Conciliation Committee can be convened to agree a joint text. If no joint text is approved then the measure either lapses or the Council can adopt it on a unilateral basis unless an absolute majority of the Parliament moves to reject the text.

The Article 189b procedure is used for internal market legislation which used to be subject to the co-operation procedure (see above). In addition it applies to the following areas:

- consumer protection;
- trans-European networks;
- some environmental measures;
- incentive measures in the field of culture;
- adoption of a multinational framework programme for research.

Assent procedure

The assent procedure was introduced by the Single European Act and can properly be called co-decision as it requires the approval of Parliament before the Council can adopt an act. Originally, the Parliament's approval was required for the admission of new members and for the conclusion of association agreements.

The category of agreements to which it applies has been considerably enlarged by the Treaty on European Union. It now applies to more international agreements and in certain cases the legislative sphere; it applies to the following:

- legislation concerning the exercise of free movement and residence rights;
- acts defining the tasks, policy objectives and organisation of structural funds;
- decision to set up a cohesion fund;
- amendment of certain provisions of the statue of ESCB;
- acts regulating elections to the European Parliament.

Budgetary powers

The Parliament's powers in relation to the budget were significantly increased by the Budgetary Treaties of 1970 and 1975. As a result of the latter Treaty the Parliament now jointly exercises control over the budget with the Council, although since 1988 it does so within the context of 'budgetary discipline'. The Council has the final say over 'compulsory expenditure' which consists mainly of expenditure on the Common Agricultural Policy; the Parliament has the final say over 'non-compulsory expenditure' which relates mainly to social and regional policy, research and aid to non-European Union countries such as Russia and countries in Eastern and Central Europe.

The powers are less impressive than they first appear. The majority of expenditure is compulsory but the proportion of non-compulsory expenditure has been increasing in recent years. There are also restrictions on the amount that non-compulsory expenditure can increase. A disagreement between the Council and Parliament as to the increase of non-compulsory expenditure lead to the ECJ annulling the adoption of the budget by the President of the Parliament in *Council v European Parliament* (1986). Since then Inter Institutional Agreements have led to the Commission, Council and Parliament agreeing 'financial perspectives' fixing annual ceilings for various categories of expenditure.

The Parliament can also reject the draft budget in its entirety and has done so on three occasions.

Special powers

The Parliament has a number of powers not directly connected with its supervisory, legislative or budgetary functions.

It has the right to approve amendments of the Treaty in the case of 'small' revisions of the ECSC Treaty.

It has power over its own internal organisation such as laying down rules of procedure. It also has the power to adopt appropriate measures to ensure the due functioning and conduct of proceedings. In case 230/81 *Luxembourg v European Parliament*, the Luxembourg government failed in its attempt to stop the Parliament dividing its plenary sessions between Luxembourg and Strasbourg. Limits were found to exist in relation to this power in case 238/81 *Luxembourg v European Parliament*, when it was held that the Parliament could only move staff to Strasbourg and Brussels to the minimum extent necessary to ensure the efficient working of the Parliament.

Parliament and the Court of Justice

Historically, the Parliament has been weak and it has constantly been attempting to extend its role and increase its power and influence. One method that the Parliament has developed of putting pressure on the Council to take decisions has been to take it to the ECJ.

Failure to act

In case 13/83 *European Parliament v Council*, the ECJ held that the Parliament could bring proceedings against the Council under Article 175 for failure to act when the Council had been in breach of its Treaty obligations because it had failed to adopt a common transport policy. Although the Court of Justice held that the Council should have acted it was not prepared to say what the content of the Council's provisions should have been.

Action to annul

Although the right to bring an action for failure to act was granted readily, there was initially far more reluctance on the part of the ECJ to allow the Parliament privileged status in bringing actions for the other type of judicial review, 'actions to annul' under Article 173. A long line of cases eg case 377/87 *European Parliament v Council* and case 302/87 *European Parliament v Council* held that the European Parliament did not have power to bring annulment proceedings. Eventually it was held in *European Parliament v Council Chernobyl* case that the Parliament could bring an action to annul where there had been an infringement of the Parliament's rights and the action was taken in order to safeguard those rights. This has now been enshrined in the Treaty, by virtue of an amendment to Article 173, introduced by the TEU.

Actions against Parliament

The Parliament can also be a defendant as well as a plaintiff before the Court of Justice. The original intention of the Treaty framers was that the Parliament should be liable for its decisions in staff cases. Liability has since been extended and the ECJ has held that the Parliament can be a source of 'justiciable acts' and can be sued under Article 173 (actions to annul), despite the fact that Article 173 does not refer to the Parliament. This has lead to other Community institutions and individuals (other than staff) challenging the decisions of the European Parliament.

So in *Parti Ecologiste 'Les Verts' v European Parliament* (1983) a French political party were able to obtain annulment of European Parliament Bureau decisions concerning the distribution of funds to political parties who participated in the 1984 Euro elections.

Similarly, in case 34/86 *Council v European Parliament* the Council obtained a ruling that the decision of the President of the Parliament declaring the 1986 budget adopted, was illegal.

The right to challenge acts of the European Parliament intended to produce legal effects *vis à vis* third parties, is now enshrined in the Treaty, by virtue of an amendment to Article 173 introduced by the TEU.

This does not mean that all acts of the Parliament are 'justiciable'. The reason the ECJ included acts of the Parliament within actions to annul, despite the original omission of the Parliament from Article 173, was to ensure that all legally binding acts were capable of judicial review. In *Group of the European Right v European Parliament* (1985) a decision by the President of the European Parliament declaring admissible a motion for the setting up of a Committee of Inquiry into the rise of fascism and racism was not capable of challenge.

Historical development of the European Parliament's powers

Examination questions frequently ask for an historical analysis of the development of the European Parliament's powers. It is important to keep certain key dates in mind.

1957
Founding Treaties give the Parliament the right to advise and be consulted, supervise the Commission and a small number of special powers.

1970/75
Budgetary Treaties give the Parliament the power to reject draft in its entirety; final say on non-compulsory expenditure and propose amendments to compulsory expenditure.

1979
Direct elections which was not an increase in powers but an enhancement of the Parliament's moral authority which encouraged the Parliament to use existing draconian powers ie rejection of draft budget, to pressurise other institutions.

1986
This year saw the introduction of the Single European Act and the introduction of the co-operation procedure. Co-decision for assent to new members and association agreements; *but* greater implementation powers for Commission, research and development (see below).

1993

Treaty on European Union. More consultative powers. Co-operation procedure extended to new powers. Introduction of procedure referred to in Article 189b. Assent extended to new areas including legislative field.

The power of veto over appointment of new Commissioners. Rigth to establish 'Committees of Inquiry'. The right to 'request' proposals from the Commission. Right of citizens of European Union to petition Parliament. Power to appoint Ombudsman. Consultative role in relation to the foreign and security and justice and home affairs pillars of the Union.

The European Parliament started as a very weak body but has steadily been increasing its powers. Successive Treaties have augmented its powers with the possible exception of the Single European Act. Bieber et al (1986) 23 CMLRev 767 argue that although powers are increased in some ways by the Single European Act in particular in relation to the decision making process, the overall effect was neutral. As the Parliament has certain 'horizontal' powers over the whole of the Treaty they argued that the effect of the Treaty on the Parliament could only be assessed by considering changes in the powers of the other institutions. The increase in the implementing powers of the Commission affected the Parliament, firstly, as the committee system (whereby the Council retains some measure of control over implementing legislation) affects the Parliament in its supervisory capacity and secondly, because the committee system weakens the Parliament's budgetary powers.

Budgetary powers are further weakened by the Single European Act as the total amounts for the technological and scientific framework programme are set by the Council after consulting the Parliament.

Although the Parliament gives the outward appearance of being like any other Parliament, the reality is quite different. Despite being the sole Community institution which had its members elected on a Euro-wide level, sovereignty still has a role to play. There are *pro rata* far fewer MEPs for the larger Member States than the smaller.

The Parliament has weak supervisory powers over the Council. The Council's decisions are taken in secret and its lack of accountability has lead to what has been called a 'democratic deficit' in the Community.

Court of Auditors

The Court of Auditors received the status of an institution by virtue of the Treaty on European Union.

Composition

There are 12 members appointed by the Council by the Council after consulting the European Parliament for renewable terms of six years. Members of the Court must have relevant auditing experience and must be independent. They may be removed from office by the ECJ if it is satisfied that the conditions and obligations of office are not met.

Role

The function of the Court of Auditors is to examine the revenue and expenditure of the Community and of bodies set up by the Community to ensure that all revenue has been received and all expenditure incurred in a lawful and regular manner and that all financial management is sound. So, it not only assesses the financial soundness of operations but also ensures that the means employed are the most economic and efficient. They will make spot checks amongst the Member States as well as the Community institutions. In the Member States the audit is carried out in liaison with the national audit bodies or national departments, who shall inform the Court of Auditors as to whether they intend to take part in the audit.

The institutions of the Community have the right to seek the opinion of the Court of Auditors on specific questions and the Court of Auditors can submit observations at any time on specific points.

The Court of Auditors produce an annual report which the institutions reply to.

The courts

European Court of Justice

Under Article 164 the function of the ECJ is to ensure that, in the interpretation and application of the Treaty, the law is observed.

Composition

Judges and Advocates General
The ECJ consists of 13 judges and six Advocates General. They must be independent and possess the qualifications required for the appointment to the highest judicial office in their respective countries

or who are juriconsults of recognised competence. They are appointed by common accord of the governments of the Member States for a term of six years, expiring at intervals of three years, although they may be re-appointed. A judge can only be removed during his term if all the judges and Advocates General are agreed.

Every Member State has a judge on the Court. The intention is that the judge will represent the legal tradition of that particular Member State rather than represent the Member State itself. There are an uneven number of judges to prevent deadlock. The extra judge comes from one of the five larger States in alphabetical order. The judges elect a President of the ECJ from among their number for a renewable term of three years.

The ECJ may sit in plenary session or in chambers which consist of three to five judges. A *quorum* of a full court consists of seven judges. Most of the caseload is dealt with by chambers but all preliminary references go before a full court and all cases where an institution or Member State so requests.

The Advocate General's position is curious to UK lawyers. The role was based on the *commissaire du gouvernement* in the French *Conseil d'Etat*. He has the same status as a judge and his duty is to present an impartial and reasoned opinion on the case, prior to the judges' deliberations. There is a slight resemblance to the *amicus curiae* in English law. An *amicus curiae* is a friend of the Court who gives the Court the benefit of his views on a question of law. A major difference between the two is that the Advocate General, in contrast to the *amicus curiae*, does not represent a particular interest and is completely independent. The opinion is usually, but not always, followed by the Court and the opinions have no legal force. The Advocate General can only hope to influence the Court through the force of his judgment as he does not take part in the judges' deliberations. It has been suggested that as the ECJ was a court of both first and last instance when it was established the Advocate General's opinion provided an in-built appeal mechanism to the ECJ's deliberations.

Legal secretaries

All judges and Advocates General have two legal secretaries who will be qualified lawyers and help the judge or Advocate General prepare his or her case.

Registrar

The ECJ is served by a registry, headed by a Registrar. His functions are twofold:

- He is involved in the judicial function of the Court. Under his supervision a register is kept in which all pleadings and supporting documents are entered in the order in which they are lodged.
- The Registrar also plays a role in the internal administration of the Court, he is responsible for the administration, financial management and accounts of the Court.

Procedure

Procedure before the Court of Justice has four stages (although the second is often ommitted):

- written proceedings;
- investigation or preparatory inquiry;
- oral proceedings;
- judgment.

Proceedings are commenced by written application. The application can be in one of 10 official or working languages of the Community. If the applicant is a Member State or individual the general rule is that the applicant has the choice of language. If the action is against the Member State the defendant chooses the language of the case. French is the working language of the Court.

The defendant serves a defence in reply to the application and it is possible for the applicant to serve a reply.

One of the judges is assigned the role of judge-rapporteur and will study the papers relating to the case, which will also have been examined by the Advocate General. After close of pleadings the ECJ may decide that a preliminary inquiry is needed, although this is rare, the decision will be based on the judge-rapporteur's preliminary report and the views of the Advocate General.

Prior to the oral hearing the judge-rapporteur issues a report summarising the facts and the parties' arguments. There are tight time limits on counsel during oral proceedings and the main speeches are not normally interrupted by questions. The Advocate General's opinion is also given orally but usually at a different time to the Counsel's arguments.

Only one judgment is produced after the judge-rapporteur has produced another report on the law relating to the case. Deliberations are in secret and the requirement to produce one judgment means that it is often anodyne where there has been disagreement between the judges, as it has to be sufficiently vague to promote agreement between them all. Judgments also tend to be bland for linguistic reasons.

The Court is bound to include, in its judgment, a decision as to costs. The usual rule is for the winning party to pay the losing party's costs but there can be exceptions such as staff cases, where the employer normally pays. Costs in preliminary references are normally reserved to the national court.

The Court can also grant legal aid. The Court will grant legal aid where it seems just and equitable to do so and it can be granted even where it it would not be available in national proceedings.

Jurisdiction

The jurisdiction of the ECJ has been conferred on it by Article 164, as follows:

- actions against institutions, including actions for annulment (Article 173); actions for failure to act (Article 175); actions for damages (Articles 178 and 215) and at one time staff cases, which are now dealt with by the Court of First Instance;
- preliminary rulings which are interlocutory references by a national court for a ruling on questions of interpretation of Treaties and secondary legislation and questions of validity of secondary legislation;
- actions brought either by the Commission (Article 169) or a Member State (Article 170) against another Member State for failure to fulfil Community obligations;
- since 1989 the ECJ has had an appellate jurisdiction and hears appeals from the Court of First Instance on points of law;
- the Court can also give advisory opinions under Article 228 on an agreement between the European Union and third countries or international organisations.

Quasi legislative role

One of the striking contrasting features of the ECJ is its approach to interpretation. The ECJ often employs a purposive or teleological approach and interprets legislation in accordance with its aims and purposes. In this approach the Court is guided by the principle of *effetutile* or effectiveness and is constantly striving to ensure that their interpretation leads to a furthering of the integration process by ensuring that the European legal order functions more effectively. It is argued that the judges are not being creative at all; that they are precluded from performing a legislative function, as they are tied to the aims of the Treaties and are therefore limited in their policy choices as a result. A problem with this analysis is that there is no unanimous agreement between the Member States as to the form integration and consequently the policy choices should take.

The teleological approach has had several important consequences. Firstly, it has lead to a constitutionalisation of the founding Treaties. This constitution is said to rest on the 'twin pillars' of direct effect and supremacy. The principle of direct effect was established in *Van Gend en Loos* (1963) which held that a Treaty article could be relied on by an individual against a national government before a national court.

The principle of supremacy was established in *Costa v ENEL* (1964) and provides that where national law and EC law conflict, then EC law shall prevail.

The ECJ has defined the powers of the respective institutions and the competence of the Community. In *Commission v Council 'ERTA'* case (1971) it was held that only the Community had competence to enter into an agreement with third countries when policy making in a certain area has been handed over to the Community.

The principle of *effet utile* in combination with Article 5 under which Member States agree to fulfil their Community obligations, have been used by the ECJ to develop an interpretive obligation on Member States (*Von Colson and Kamann* (1986) and *Marleasing* (1990)); and the safeguarding of rights through the availability of compensation in the event of the State breaching those rights (*Francovich* (1990)).

The ECJ has also been involved in negative integration, ie the removal of barriers to trade. It has defined the obligations of the Member States in relation to free movement of goods, persons and capital.

Easson feels that the activist stage of the ECJ has come to an end and that now the general principles of the legal order are established then further developments will depend on the legislators. On the other hand, Ramussen feels that the ECJ has been unnecessarily activist in the past and will continue to be so in the future. Ramussen and Snyder see a danger in the ECJ's activist role as it has led to a lack of popular involvement in the development of the legal order.

Court of First Instance

The case load of the ECJ has increased dramatically since the inception of the Community. It can now take up to two years to receive a judgment. To help alleviate the workload the Single European Act provided for the establishment of a Court of First Instance. The CFI was established by Council Decision 88/591 and began hearing cases in 1989.

The CFI consists of 12 judges and sits in chambers of three or five judges or occasionally in plenary session. There are no specially appointed Advocates General but a judge can be called upon to perform the function in a particular case. Article 168(a)(3) provides that to qualify as judges

...members of [the] court shall be chosen from persons whose independence is beyond doubt and who possess the ability required for appointment to judicial office.

There is a President of the Court who is elected from amongst the judges. The CFI has its own Registry and the members of the Court have their own personal staff but otherwise all other services are provided by the staff of the ECJ.

Under Article 3 of the decision, the CFI's jurisdiction was laid down, as follows:

- staff cases;
- actions brought by coal and steel undertakings under the ECSC Treaty;
- actions brought by natural and legal persons against a Community institution under Article 173(2) or Article 175(3) relating to the implementation of competition rules applicable to undertakings (excluding preliminary references);
- since June 1993, all claims brought by 'natural and legal persons' under Articles 173 and 175 (except anti-dumping cases);
- since March 1994, all anti-dumping cases brought by natural and legal persons have been transferred.

The competition and staff cases take up most of the CFI's time. Both types of case are fact-based and were therefore thought suitable to transfer to a different court as they would be the most likely to alleviate workload. It has always been envisaged that there will be further transfers of jurisdiction to the CFI and under a Treaty on European Union amendment the 'classes of action or proceeding' coming within the CFI's jurisdiction (with the exception of preliminary references) are left open, to be decided by the Council at the request of the ECJ.

It is possible to appeal a decision of the CFI to the ECJ, on points of law only, on three grounds:

- the lack of competence of the CFI;
- the breach of procedure before the CFI which adversely affects the interests of the applicant;
- the infringement of Community law by the CFI.

If the ECJ finds that an appeal is successful, it quashes the CFI's judgment. It can then give final judgment itself or refer the case back to the CFI for judgment.

Kennedy 14 (1989) EL Rev 7 saw a danger that if a high proportion of CFI decisions ended in appeals, then there would be a minimal reduction in the ECJ's caseload. However, even of this were to occur then the ECJ would still save time as the facts have already been determined by the CFI leaving the ECJ to apply the law.

Since the inception of the CFI there has been little reduction in the waiting time before the ECJ, as it coincided with an increase in cases.

Subsidiary bodies

Economic and Social Committee

The Economic and Social Committee represents all sectors of economic and social life such as employers, trade unions, consumer groups and the professions. It is not an institution in the formal sense. It is an advisory committee and must be consulted by the Council or Commission when required. It is also entitled on its own initiative to prepare reports on specific fields.

The effectiveness of the Committee has been limited. Its opinions do not have to be followed and it tends to speak with a discordant voice the result of its members representing conflicting interests and consequently taking opposing viewpoints.

Committee of Regions

The Treaty on European Union created a Committee of Regions which also acts in an advisory capacity. It is made up of representatives of 'regional and local bodies' so that decisions can be taken 'as closely as possible to the people'.

European Investment Bank

The European Investment Bank is the Union's long term lending bank and the regional development bank for Europe. It makes grants and loans for projects for developing poorer regions, modernising or converting undertakings or developing new activities within the common market, or projects of common interest to several Member States which are of such a size or nature they cannot be financed entirely by various sources available in the individual Member States.

Revision Notes

The Commission

Functions

Initiator of Community action

The Commission has historically had the right of legislative initiative. This role has been diluted by the TEU:

- the European Parliament can 'request' proposals;
- the right to submit proposals is shared with Member States in respect to common security and foreign policy;
- the Commission only has the right of initiative in respect of some matters in relation to judicial and home affairs.

Community watchdog

Articles 169-170
The Commission has a central role in informal proceedings under both Articles 169 and 170 enforcement proceedings.

Competition law
The Commission is the watchdog of the Community's competition policy and has the power to impose fines and penalties.

Executive of the Community

The Commission has a small primary legislative function (*France, Italy and UK v Commission* (1980)). The Commission has been given wide powers of delegated legislation.

Recommendations and opinions

The Commission can formulate recommendations and opinions on matters dealt with in the Treaty.

Representative, financial and administrative functions

The Commission has a wide number of representative, administrative and financial functions.

Composition

The composition of the Commission is as follows:

- 17 Commissioners;
- one President;
- one-two Vice Presidents;
- 23 Directorates General.

Directorates General are sub-divided into Directorates, which in turn are made up of divisions. Each Commissioner is assisted by a *Cabinet* which is headed by a *Chef de Cabinet*.

Council of European Union

Functions

- takes general policy decisions;
- ensures Treaty objectives are attained;
- ensures co-ordination of general economic policies;
- power to take decisions;
- concludes agreements with third countries;
- jointly decides budget.

Composition

The Council is not a fixed body but each Member State is represented by a government minister who has responsibility for the subject matter of the meeting.

The Presidency rotates amongst the Council at six monthly intervals.

The Council is assisted by permanent representatives from each country. The Committee of Permanent Representatives is known as COREPER who carry out the work of the Ministers in their absence in their own country.

Voting

A few matters are dealt with unanimously. A few unimportant matters are dealt with by a simple majority. Most matters are dealt with by a qualified majority, with the larger countries having more votes than the smaller countries.

European Council

Meetings of the Heads of State and government are supposed to provide the Community with the necessary impetus to move it forward politically.

European Parliament

Supervisory function

The Parliament supervises the work of the Commission.

Participation in legislative process

The Parliament has four different modes of participating in the legislative process:

- consultation procedure;
- co-operation procedure;
- co-decision procedure;
- assent.

The relevant procedure and consequently the Parliament's involvement in the process is governed by the Treaties.

Budgetary powers

The Parliament jointly decides the budget with the Council. The Council has the final say over compulsory expenditure and the Parliament has the final say over non-compulsory expenditure and can reject the budget in its entirety.

Special powers

The Parliament has a small number of special powers:

- approve small amendments to the ECSC Treaty;
- power over its own internal organisation.

Parliament and Court of Justice

The Court of Justice has held that the Parliament can bring an action for failure to act (*European Parliament v Council* (1983)). It can also bring an action to annul where there has been an infringement of its rights and the action is intended to protect those rights (*European Parliament v Council 'Chernobyl'* case (1988)).

Court of Auditors

The Court of Auditors has been made a full institution of the Community in the TEU.

Court of Justice

Composition

The Court of justice consists of 13 judges and six Advocates General; they elect a President amongst themselves. The Court may sit in a plenary session or in chambers of three or five judges.

Jurisdiction

The Court of Justice hears the following cases:

- actions against institutions;
- preliminary rulings;
- enforcement proceedings;
- appeals from the Court of First Instance and appeals from undertakings fined by the Commission;
- advisory opinions.

Quasi legislative role

The Court of Justice uses a purposive or teleological approach to interpretation. In using this approach it is guided by the principle of *effet utile* or effectiveness and it strives to ensure that its interpretation furthers the integrative process by ensuring that the European legal order functions more effectively.

Court of First Instance

This was created in 1989 to help the ECJ with its increasing workload. It has a limited jurisdiction and appeals can be made on points of law to the ECJ.

4 Free movement of goods

You should be familiar with the following areas: ✓

- principles of a Customs Union (Article 9) free trade area, Common Customs Tariff and Article 115

- prohibition of customs duties and charges having equivalent effect on imports and exports (Articles 12-17)

- discriminatory internal taxation (Article 95)

- elimination of quantitative restrictions and measures having equivalent effect on imports and exports (Article 30 and Art 34)

- Directive 70/50

- distinctly and indistinctly applicable measures – the *Dassonville* formula

- 'mandatory' requirements, the rule of reason and 'necessary' measures – *Cassis de Dijon*

- principle of mutual recognition – *Cassis de Dijon*

- derogations from free movement principle in particular: Article 36 – derogations from Articles 30-34 and Article 115

Historical background

The EC is a form of economic integration, combining elements of a custom union, a common market, common economic policies and the Treaty on European Union provides for economic and monetary union. Central to these aims and objectives is the free movement of goods which has both an internal and external aspect.

The external aspect provides for a customs union. The internal aspect consists of provisions regarding customs duties and equivalent charges, domestic taxation and quantitative restrictions and equivalent measures.

The purpose behind these provisions is the removal of all internal barriers to trade within the Community and a common commercial front to the outside world.

The Single European Act introduced Article 8(a) (which has become Article 7(a) following the coming into force of the Treaty on European Union) which provides for the creation of an internal market and comprises an area without internal frontiers in which free movement of *inter alia* goods is ensured. It also provides that under Article 100(a) qualified voting would exist in the Council of Ministers where one of the internal market objectives is being achieved.

A Treaty creating a European Economic Area has been concluded between EC countries, EFTA countries (with the exception of Switzerland, due to a negative vote in a referendum). The position under this agreement is very similar to that which exists under the EC Treaty with similar aims and objectives and similar provisions relating to the free movement of goods. The Treaty came into force on 1 January 1994.

The Treaty on European Union reproduces similar provisions to those which already exist under the EC Treaty, as far as free movement of goods is concerned, but there will be greater ease of free movement through the establishment of an Economic and Monetary Union.

Customs Union

Article 9 of the Treaty provides that the Community 'shall be based upon a customs union'.

A customs union consists of two parts:

- a free trade area consisting of a group of territories where duties have been eliminated;
- a common tariff is adopted in trade relations with the outside world.

A common tariff is considered an essential part of a customs union, under Article 10 goods from non-Member States which have complied with formalities and have paid customs duties are regarded as being in 'free circulation' in the Community and have the same freedom of movement as goods which have originated in the Community. Unless every country had the same tariff with regard to goods entering from non-Member States it would be possible to shop around and find a country with a low tariff. Once this low tariff had been paid goods would circulate freely around the Community.

Common Customs Tariff (CCT)

As part of its common commercial policy and in order to ensure equal treatment in all Member States for goods imported into the EC from non-Member States, the Treaty provides for the introduction of a Common Customs Tariff (CCT). It applies to all products imported into the Community from outside the EC.

The operation of the CCT is governed by Articles 18-29. Once goods are imported into the Community the free movement provisions apply. The tariffs raised under the CCT form part of the Community's own resources for the purposes of the Community budget.

A single external tariff was introduced on 1 July 1968. The only way in which imported goods can be denied free movement amongst the Community is if the Commission has authorised a derogation in the event of economic difficulties or deflection of trade in any Member State resulting from the implementation of commercial policy under Article 115. This derogation only applies insofar as the Common Commercial Policy is incomplete.

Member States cannot impose charges in excess of CCT
The EC Treaty makes no express prohibition on Member States imposing charges equivalent to customs duties on imports from non-Member States after the Common Customs Tariff has entered into force. This is in contrast to goods originating in Member States and moving between Member States where not only are customs duties prohibited but also charges having equivalent effect. However, it is clear from *Diamantarbeiders v Indiamex* (1973) that Member States cannot impose charges on goods from third countries which supplement the Common Customs Tariff.

Member States can charge for mandatory inspections
A Member State is allowed to hold and charge for health inspections where they could be held and charged for in internal Community trade (*Simmenthal v Italian Finance Administration* (1978)).

Such charges can be in excess of those carried out for internal Community trade provided that the cost in not disproportionate.

No discriminatory internal taxation
Member States cannot impose discriminatory internal taxes on goods in 'free circulation' (*Co-Frutta* (1987)).

Quantitative restrictions and measures having equivalent effect
It was said in *Donckerwolke v Procureur de la République de Lille* (1976) that the provisions of Article 30 relating to elimination of quantitative

restrictions and measures having equivalent effect apply to goods in 'free circulation'. This approach was followed in *Tezi Textiel v Commission* (1986).

Scope of the provisions on free movement

The meaning of 'goods'

It was held in *Commission v Italy* (1968) 'the art treasures case' that goods of an historic or artistic interest were goods within the meaning of the Treaty, as they had a monetary value and could constitute the object of commercial transactions.

Television broadcasts are a service

The supply of television broadcasts was held to be a 'service not a good' in *Procureur du Roi v Debauve* (1980), although this has been criticised.

Means of payment are not goods

In *R v Thompson* (1978) the ECJ developed a distinction between 'goods' and 'means of payment'. UK rules prohibit the export of silver coins minted before 1947 and it was held that free movement of goods rules did not apply to 'means of payment'. As the coins were minted before 1947 they were no longer a 'means of payment' but were goods. An export ban was held to be justified as the destruction of the coins was illegal.

Goods in free circulation

Once goods from third countries have paid the Common Customs Tariff they are then in 'free circulation' and enjoy the same benefits as if they had originated in the Community.

The Irish government could not, therefore, demand that potatoes which had been imported into the UK from Cyprus and re-exported to Ireland obtain a licence (*Commission v Ireland* (Cyprus potatoes) (1985)).

Who is bound?

The parties who may be subject to these provisions:

* The Community is bound not to act contrary to these provisions: *Ravel* (1978); *Rivoria* (1979); *Migliorini* (1985); *REWE Zentrale* (1984); *Denkavit Nederland* (1984); *Bauhuis v Netherlands* (1977).

- The Member States are the principal addresses. This covers governmental, regional and local authorities, acts of national courts and public bodies of various kinds. It also includes acts of bodies which are not part of the State machinery whose acts may be regarded as assumed by, or attributable to, the State, even if the acts are not binding.

The term Member State includes a private body which receives sponsorship from the State *(Commission v Ireland* (Buy Irish*)* (1982)). The Irish government supported a 'Buy Irish' campaign to persuade people to buy Irish goods and they were held to be in breach of the Treaty. The campaign had been manifestly unsuccessful as the percentage of Irish goods bought during the campaign went down.

A privatised utility company is regarded as an 'entity of the State' and bound by the provisions *(Foster v British Gas* (1990)).

It is generally thought that the free movement of goods provisions are not of horizontal effect.

Initially the ECJ thought that agreements between undertakings could be caught by the free movement of goods provisions. In *Dansk Supermarked v Imerco* (1981) it was held that it is impossible in any circumstances for agreements between individuals to derogate from the mandatory provisions of the Treaty on the free movement of goods.

More recently the court has consistently taken a different line. It was suggested *(obiter)* in *Officier van Justitie v Van de Haar* (1984) that the free movement of goods provisions were not addressed to individual undertakings or associations.

Despite this *dicta* there still remains a possibility that actions by an individual may still be subject to the free movement of goods provisions but certainly not if the individual is acting outside a legal context *(Apple and Pear Development Council v Lewis* (1983)). A producer, or a producer's association which is a voluntary undertaking, may advertise or promote national products on the basis of their national origin provided public finance is not used.

Customs duties and equivalent charges

This is governed by Articles 12-17.

Article 12 is the 'standstill' provision, prohibiting the introduction of *new* customs duties or charges of equivalent effect on imports and exports.

Articles 13-15 provides for abolition of existing duties (or equivalent) on *imports* within certain time limits, known as the transitional period.

Article 16 provides for abolition on such duties and charges on *exports*.

Charges having equivalent effect to customs duties

A charge need not be introduced for protectionist reasons and will include any charge which is imposed on goods by reason of the fact that it has crossed a frontier. In *Diamantarbeiders* (1969) a charge had been imposed for reasons of social policy but was still found to be illegal.

'Genuine' taxes fall outside Articles 12-16

A charge of equivalent effect to a customs duty may come in many guises, including a tax. Genuine taxes fall under Article 95 but if it is not a genuine tax it will come within Articles 12-16. This poses great problems in determining whether a 'tax' is genuine or a charge having equivalent effect to a customs duty.

In *Commission v France* (reprographic machines) (1981) a genuine tax was defined as one 'relating to a general system of internal dues applied systematically to categories of products in accordance with objective criteria irrespective of the origin of the products'. Therefore, for a tax to be genuine it must be part of an overall system of taxation and not superimposed with a particular purpose in mind.

Charges imposed for the benefit of the importer

A charge of equivalent effect includes a charge levied in order to benefit the importer (*Commission v Italy* (statistical levy) (1969)). A levy was applied to all imports and exports, regardless of source, and the proceeds were used to finance an export statistical service for the benefit of importers and exporters but it was found to be a charge having equivalent effect. Its advantages are held to be so general and uncertain that it could not be considered as a payment for services rendered.

Charges for services rendered

A charge for a service rendered is permissible but this principle has been interpreted very narrowly.

In *Donner* (1983), an importer of books was faced with a demand for a charge levied by the Dutch Post Office for having dealt with the payment of value added tax on importation and he argued that this was a charge for the purpose of customs duties.

The ECJ said the national court should consider how realistic it was for the individual recipient to deal with payment of value added tax himself and how much it would have cost him. If, in the light of this, the charge was reasonable, it could be regarded as payment for service rendered.

The charge must be related to the service provided. The Spanish authorities in *Ford España v Spain* (location of customs formalities) (1989) argued that it was a service to the importer to allow customs formalities to be carried out at the place of destination rather than at the frontier. It was held that the charge did not relate to a specific service as it was levied on a flat rate basis.

Customs formalities completed within normal hours cannot be considered a service (*Commission v Italy* (customs hours) (1989)). The Italian government argued that to allow frontier formalities to be carried out outside certain defined times was a service for which a charge could be made. However, the Italians wished to make a charge in respect of times when the borders were required to be open under Community law, so the charge was not permissible.

In a later case, *Commission v Italy* (extraordinary customs clearance) (1993) it was held that although charges for customs formalities conducted outside normal hours or normal premises was a service rendered that the charge must be proportionate to the service.

Charges relating to requirements of Community law

Charges for inspections are not permissible unless they are mandatory under Community law.

Consequently, it is not possible to charge for an inspection which is permitted but not mandatory under Community law (*Commission v Belgium* (health inspection service) (1985)).

This can be contrasted with the situation where the inspection is required under Community law (*Bauhuis* (1977)). Proceedings were brought by a cattle dealer to recover fees for veterinary inspections. Some of the inspections were required by Community law while others were required by national law.

The inspections imposed by the Directive were intended for the good of the Community as a whole and charges were permissible provided they did not exceed the actual cost of the inspection. The inspections required by the Dutch law alone were unilateral obstacles to the free movement of goods and were therefore equivalent to customs duties.

Mandatory inspections under international conventions

The theory is that inspections under Community law obviate the need for national inspections and therefore promote the free movement of goods, enabling Member States to recover the cost of them. The same approach has been adopted with regard to international conventions, at least to the extent that the need for unilateral national inspections is removed.

In *Commission v Netherlands* (1977), it was held that fees could be charged for inspections carried out under the 1951 International Plant Protection Convention to which all Member States were a party, as they helped promote free movement of goods.

Charges falling within the scope of internal taxation

Internal taxation is only unlawful to the extent that it is discriminatory against imported products or protective of domestic products.

The ECJ has held that where a charge is levied both on imports and exports, it can still be a charge equivalent to a customs duty. This causes difficulties in deciding whether the charge is equivalent to a customs duty, and comes within Articles 12-16, or is internal taxation and therefore comes within Article 95.

In *Cucchi v Avez* (1977) it was said that, internal taxation will only constitute a charge equivalent to a customs duty 'if it has the sole purpose of financing activities for the specific advantage of the taxed domestic product'. The taxed product and the product benefiting must also be the same and the charges imposed on the domestic product have been made good in full.

In the cases *Demoor Gilbert en Zonenv Belgium* (1993); *Lornoy v Belgium* (1993) and *Openbaar Ministerie v Clareys* (1993) charges were imposed on domestic products and imports alike and the proceeds were paid to funds that benefited the domestic product. It was held that where the charge is paid solely for the benefit of a domestic product and the resulting benefits offset the charge as far as the domestic product is concerned it is a charge having equivalent effect to a customs duty within Article 12. Where the benefits accruing to the domestic product only partly offset the effect of the charge then it is a discriminatory tax within Article 95.

A charge only constitutes internal taxation if it is levied on the same chargeable event for imports and domestic products. In *Denkavit Loire v France* (1979) a charge on the import of lard was claimed by French authorities to equate to a domestic charge on the slaughter of a pig. It was felt that this levelled the playing field but the charge on the lard was equivalent to a customs duty. It could not come within the provision on internal taxation as there were different chargeable events.

Internal taxation

The prohibition on discriminatory taxation is contained in the tax provisions of the Treaty under Article 95 and not with the provisions which relate to free movement of goods, however, it is usually considered alongside these provisions.

Articles 12-15 and Article 95 are mutually exclusive

It was held in *Cucchi v Avez Spa* (1977) that the prohibition on customs duties and charges having equivalent effect and discriminatory internal taxation are mutually exclusive and so it is best to involve Article 12 and Article 95, in cases of doubt.

A 'genuine tax' is a measure relating to a system of internal dues applied systematically to categories of products in accordance with objective criteria irrespective of the origin of the products (*Commission v France* (reprographic machines) (1981)).

The purpose of Article 95

The ECJ has stated that Article 95 is calculated to close any loopholes which internal taxation might open in the prohibition on customs duties and charges having equivalent effect. It was held to be directly effective in *Lütticke* (1966).

Third country products

Article 95 only expressly refers to products 'of' Member States and does not refer to products of third countries in 'free circulation' in the Community.

Nevertheless, Article 95 was held to apply to third country goods in 'free circulation' in *Co-Frutta* (1987).

Similar domestic products/indirect protection

The first paragraph of Article 95 states that:

... no Member State shall impose, directly or indirectly, on the products of other Member States any internal taxation of any kind in excess of that imposed directly or indirectly on *similar* domestic products.

The important point is that the goods do not need to be identical, they only need to be *similar.*

The term *similar* must be interpreted widely. It was defined in *Commission v France* (taxation of spirits) (1980) as those which meet the same needs from the point of view of consumers and are broadly in competition with each other.

French legislation imposed a higher duty on grain based spirits than on fruit based spirits. This breached Community law as the grain based spirits (whisky, gin etc) were imported and French production was of fruit based spirit.

Taxation policy must not be allowed to crystallise consumer habits and must also take into account likely future developments in the market. In *Commission v United Kingdom* (excise duties on wine) (1980) beer and wine were subject to different rates of tax in the UK but they were to be regarded as *similar* products. There was a competitive relationship between beer and 'accessible' wines and there should be fair competition between them.

So, in addition to the requirements not to impose a discriminatory tax on similar products, there is a similar requirement not to impose a discriminatory tax on goods that compete with each other.

Directly or indirectly

Article 95 para 1, prohibits internal taxation of any kind in excess of that imposed directly *or indirectly* on similar domestic products.

The ECJ has said that the term 'directly or indirectly' was to be construed broadly and includes all taxation levied on raw materials and semi-finished products incorporated in the goods in question (*Molkerei-Zentrale v Hauptzollmat Paderborn* (1968)). However, the effect of the charges diminishes with each stage of production and distribution and their effect becomes negligible.

The court defined 'indirect taxation' as all taxation specifically imposed on the domestic product at the earlier stage of production.

Ancillary services

Article 95 also extends to taxation of services ancillary to the supply of goods. *Schöttle v FZA Freudenstedt* (1977) concerned a German tax on the transport of goods by road. The tax was charged on a different basis for the international carriage of goods than for purely domestic transport. In some cases the product could be transported the same distance within Germany and would be subject to less tax than if the border had been crossed. This was discriminatory.

Taxes applicable in practice only to imports

The court have had to consider the problem of whether it is discriminatory or protective to tax an imported product for which there is no domestic equivalent.

In *Fink-Frucht* (sweet peppers) (1968) the ECJ held that where the Member State did not import the goods in question they had nothing to protect, therefore, a tax could not be discriminatory.

This can be contrasted with *Humblot* (French cars) (1985), where there was no identical product to protect but there were competing products. France imposed two types of annual tax on motor vehicles. Cars of less than 16 CV were subject to a lower tax than cars in excess of 16 CV. France did not manufacture cars in excess of 16 CV and therefore the tax was held to be discriminatory and contrary to Article 95.

Justifiable difference in treatment

The ECJ has been prepared to allow higher taxation of products even where the category of products is largely imported, if the differential can be objectively justified, provided the economic policy objectives are compatible with the requirements of Community law and there are detailed rules to prevent discrimination and protection.

In *Vinal v Orbat* (1981) Italy taxed alcohol derived from petroleum at a higher rate than alcohol derived from fermentation. This was held to be a legitimate choice of industrial policy and could not be considered discriminatory. Although it affected imports from Members States it also had an affect in Italy where it hampered the establishment of the alcohol.

Quantitative restrictions/measures having equivalent effect

The abolition of customs duties and charges of equivalent effect alone would not have been sufficient to guarantee the free movement of goods within the common market. In addition to pecuniary restrictions there are restrictions of a non-pecuniary nature which can hinder the free flow of goods. Consequently, Article 30 which eliminates quantitative restrictions and measures having equivalent effect, is the central provision of the Treaty relating to the free movement of goods.

The principal provisions are:

* Article 30, which prohibits quantitative restrictions, and all measures having equivalent effect on *imports;*
* Article 34, which contains a similar prohibition on *exports;*
* Articles 31-33 which provide for the gradual abolition of import restrictions during the transitional period.

Article 36 provides for derogations from Articles 30-34.

Direct effect of Article 30

Article 30, 'the standstill provision' was held to be directly effective in *Salgoil v Italian Ministry of Foreign Affairs* (1968). Articles 34 and 36 by analogy must also have direct effect.

No *de minimis* rule

In contrast to the rules relating to competition Articles 30-36 are not subject to any *de minimis* rule regarding effect (*Prantl* (1984)) and *Van de Haar* (1984)).

Quantitative restrictions

A quantitative restriction is a national measure which places physical/non pecuniary restrictions on the amount of goods that may enter or leave the Member State. The most common example is a quota.

In *Geddo v Ente Nazionale Risi* (1973) it was said that:

the prohibition of quantitative restrictions covers measures which amount to a total or partial restraint of according to the circumstances, imports, exports or goods in transit.

Quantitative restrictions are not as prevalent as measures having equivalent effect but the following have been held to have come within the definition of quantitative restrictions: suspension of pork imports (*Commission v Italy* (ban on pork imports) (1961)); a ban on pornographic literature but subject to the derogations of Article 36 (*R v Henn and Darby* (1979)); a quota system (*Salgoil SpA* (1968)) and a licensing system might amount to a quantitative restriction or more likely, a measure having equivalent effect (*International Fruit Co NV Produktschap vor Groenten en Fruit* (1971)).

Measures

The concept of measures has been widely interpreted by the ECJ and also the Commission.

Government sponsorship for a 'Buy Irish' campaign was held to be a 'measure' in *Commission v Ireland* (Buy Irish) (1982).

However, measures taken by an individual who is not acting in a legal context probably falls outside the rules (*Apple and Pear Development Council v Lewis* (1983)).

Having equivalent effect

The Commission's interpretation of Article 30 can be found in Directive 70/50 which makes an important distinction between measures applicable only to imports ('distinctly applicable') and measures applicable to domestic and imported products alike ('indistinctly applicable').

As a general rule the Commission did not feel that 'indistinctly applicable' measures came within Article 30. Nevertheless Article 3 sets out a number of concrete cases where 'indistinctly applicable' measures constitute abuse:

... measures governing the marketing of products which deal, in particular, with shape, size, weight, composition, presentation, identification or putting up and which are equally applicable to domestic and imported products, where the restrictive effect of such measures on the free movement of goods exceeds the effects intrinsic to trade rules.

The ECJ introduced its own definition of measures having equivalent effect to quantitative restrictions in *Procureur du Roi v Dassonville* (1974):

All trading rules enacted by Member States which are capable of hindering directly or indirectly, actually or potentially, intra-Community trade are to be considered as measures having an effect equivalent to quantitative restrictions.

Two points can be noted from this definition. Firstly, it is not necessary to show an actual effect on trade between Member States as long as the measure is capable of such effects. This dispenses with the need for an economic analysis to show the effect on trade.

Secondly, it is a very wide definition, as the inclusion of the word 'indirect' brings commercial and marketing rules within its ambit where they have an effect on imports. The ECJ's definition differs from the Commission's as the ECJ includes indistinctly applicable measures but the Commission only includes them to the extent that they constitute abuse.

Distinctly applicable measures under Article 30

An example of distinctly applicable measures which applied only to imports occurred in *Commission v UK* (UHT) (1983). UK rules on the importation of UHT milk contained two main elements. The first was a requirement to obtain an import licence; the second was that the UHT milk should be packed in a dairy approved by the competent local authority, ie they should be packed in the UK, which effectively meant that the milk had to be re-treated in the UK which would make importation uneconomic. It was held that both restrictions were disproportionate and therefore, illegal.

Indistinctly applicable measures under Article 30

The wide interpretation given by the ECJ to Article 30 in *Dassonville* lead to a number of problems and the court has not always been consistent in its approach. A modifying of the approach and a change of emphasis can be seen in *Rewe-Zentrale AG v Bundesmonopolverwaltung für Branntwein* (1979) *'Cassis de Dijon'*. A German law laid down a minimum alcohol level of 25% for certain spirits, which included cassis, a blackcurrant flavoured liquor. German cassis complied with the minimum alcohol level but French cassis did not. Although the German measure was indistinctly applicable it effectively banned French cassis from the German market.

The ECJ applied the *Dassonville* formula but qualified it by applying a 'rule of reason'.

Obstacles to movement within the Community resulting from disparities between the national laws relating to the marketing of the products in question must be accepted in so far as those provisions may be recognised as being necessary in order to satisfy mandatory requirements relating, in particular, to the effectiveness of fiscal supervision, the protection of public health, the fairness of commercial transactions and the defence of the consumer.

Before *Cassis de Dijon*, it was thought that all measures breaching the *Dassonville* formula would breach Article 30 unless justified by Article 36. *Cassis* changed that rule in so far as a rule of reason could be applied to Article 30 at least for indistinctly applicable measures. The 'rule of reason' represents an equitable approach justifying certain measures until harmonising legislation is introduced. Wyatt & Dashwood point out that prior to *Cassis* the emphasis had been on establishing whether the rule was discriminatory against imports whereas *Cassis* looks to the protective effect of rules. It looks to whether the rules go beyond the interest in question to establish whether their effect is to protect domestic products.

The 'rule of reason' is known as the first *Cassis* principle. The court also established a second important principle in *Cassis de Dijon*. It suggested that while there was no valid reason why goods that have been lawfully produced and marketed in one of the Member States should not be imported into any other Member State. This leads to a presumption that goods which have been lawfully marketed in another State will comply with the mandatory requirements of the importing State. The presumption can be rebutted by evidence that further measures are necessary to protect the interest concerned. This principle of mutual recognition is a corner-stone of the internal market.

The *Cassis* approach was confirmed in *Gilli and Andres (Italian Vinegar)* (1980). National legislation prohibited the marketing of vinegar creating acetic acid derived other than from the acetic fermentation of wine. Cider vinegar did not constitute a threat to health and consumers could be protected by labelling. The ECJ found that the principal effect of the rules was to protect national production by laying down national rules which products from other Member States would not comply with.

Restrictions on trade, caused by differences in laws between Member States, would be overcome by the presumption of mutual recognition. A Member State could impose its own laws in the areas of fiscal supervision, fair competition, consumer protection and public health but only insofar as those restrictions are 'necessary'. In *Gilli & Andres* all that was necessary to protect public health was the labelling of cider vinegar and wine vinegar respectively in order to prohibit cider vinegar went beyond what was 'necessary' for the protection of health and unduly restricted trade.

The Commission produced a communication of 3 October 1990 OJ 1980 C256/2 concerning the consequences of the *Cassis* case, in which it said:

Any product imported from another Member State must in principle be admitted to the territory of the importing Member State if it has been lawfully produced, that is, conforms to rules and processes of manufacture that are customarily and traditionally accepted in the exporting country, and is marketed in the territory of another.

Unnecessary measures

Cassis only allows the imposition by a Member State of its 'mandatory requirements' to protect the interests it lists and only to the extent that is 'necessary.' If a lesser measure can protect the interest concerned and have a less restrictive effect on trade then that is all that is 'necessary'. The burden on Member States to prove that the legislation is 'necessary' has proved to be a heavy one.

Measures which have been found not 'necessary' include rules imposing a labelling requirement (*Fietje* (1980)); rules prohibiting the use of the additive nisin in cheese (*Eyssen* (1981)); rules regulating the dry matter content of bread (*Kelderman* (1981)); rules requiring silver products to be hallmarked were enforceable against imports unless they had been hallmarked differently (*Robertson* (1982)); rules requiring margarine to be sold in cube shaped packets to distinguish it from butter (*Rau* (1982)) and rules restricting or prohibiting certain forms of advertising (*Oosthoek Uitgevershaatschappij BV* (1982)). Recently, in *Rocher* (1993) a ban in German law prohibiting 'eye catching' price comparisons in advertisements was held to be disproportionate. It was only necessary to ban misleading advertisements, to ban them all was unnecessary.

Further mandatory requirements

Cassis de Dijon permitted Member States to impose their own mandatory requirements in relation to public health, consumer protection, fiscal supervision and fair competition. The list of mandatory requirements is not exhaustive and has been added to by later cases which have permitted the protection of other interests such as social policy, socio-cultural characteristics and measures for the protection of the environment.

In *Oebel* (1981) social policy, in the form of improvement of working conditions by limiting night working hours was held to be a 'mandatory requirement'.

In *Cinéthèque SA v Fédération Nationale des Cinémas Français* (1985) French legislation prohibited the sale or hire of video cassettes of a film within a fixed period from the film's release in the cinema. The ECJ found that this did restrict intra-Community trade but the restriction was justified. There was no express reference to a 'mandatory requirement' but Advocate General Slynn's opinion talked of the need to protect the European film industry. The point was not dealt with in the judgment but the case is taken as authority for protection of cultural characteristics being a 'mandatory requirement.'

'Mandatory requirements' have been extended to include the environment initially in *Association des bruleurs d'huiles usagees* (1985). This was followed in *Commission v Denmark* (Danish bottles) (1986). Danish legislation required drinks to be sold in returnable containers to help reduce litter. It was held that national legislation designed to protect the environment may be regarded as justifying intra-Community trade restrictions. Although, in this case, the measures were justifiable, in principle, certain details of the scheme were unnecessarily restrictive and could not therefore be justified.

Retail sector

Cases relating to the retail sector illustrate clearly the inconsistencies of the ECJ's approach as to what constitutes a 'trading rule' within the meaning of the *Dassonville* formula.

In *Torfaen BC v B and Q plc* (1990) a challenge was made to the British Sunday trading laws. There was some disagreement as to whether Sunday trading could constitute a 'trading rule' with Advocate General Van Gerven thinking that it could not. It was held that such measures constituted a 'legitimate part of economic and social policy' and were designed to accord with 'national or regional socio-cultural characteristics.' Sunday trading rules did not, therefore, breach Article 30 provided their 'restrictive effect did not exceed the effects intrinsic to rules of that kind' ie their restrictive effects must not be disproportionate to their purpose, and it was for the national court to decide whether the restrictive effects exceeded the aim in view.

Belgian Sunday trading laws were the subject of a reference in *Marchandise and ors* (1991). A Belgian law which prohibited the employment of workers in retail shops on Sundays after 12 noon was not disproportionate to the socio-cultural aim pursued. (The ECJ ruled on proportionality issue). Similarly, in *Conforama* (1991) the ECJ ruled again on proportionality despite having said in *Torfaen* that it was a matter for the national court to decide.

There had been unhappiness on that part of British courts that they were to rule on the question whether the Shops Act was disproportionate to the object to be achieved. So the House of Lords again made a preliminary reference in *Stoke on Trent City Council and Norwich City Council v B and Q plc* (1992). The ECJ said the fact that a particular question is one for the national court, does not endow that court with quasi-legislative powers. It had ruled on proportionality in *Conforama* and *Marchandise*, as it had all the information to make such a ruling and therefore had to do so to ensure a uniform interpretation. The ECJ again held that the effects of the British Sunday trading laws were not excessive.

The Sunday trading cases are hard to reconcile with the approach adopted in *Quietlynn and Richards v Southend Borough Council* (1990). It was held that national legislation, which only permitted the sale of sex articles from licensed sex establishments, was not a 'trading rule' within the *Dassonville* formula. Similarly, in *Blesgen* (1982) the ECJ held that a restriction on the sales outlets of spirits fell outside *Dassonville*. It is hard to see why these are not trading rules, while the Sunday trading cases do come within the definition albeit as justified exceptions.

There is disagreement amongst academic writers as to whether the 'rule of reason' creates a category of exceptions to Article 30 or whether it takes certain cases out of the ambit of Article 30 altogether.

An attempt to explain the confusion surrounding the inconsistencies in the ECJ's approach was made by White 26 (1989) CML Rev 235-280 by drawing a distinction between the circumstances surrounding the sale of a product and the characteristics of the product. Restrictions on the circumstances in which goods are marketed such as limitations on by whom, where, when, or how goods may be sold or used or at what price they may be sold do not fall within Article 30, as they do not threaten the unified market but requirements that imported goods have the same characteristics as domestic goods are caught by Article 30 unless they are necessary 'mandatory requirements' or come within Article 36 exceptions. If the circumstances relating to the sale or use of goods made their sale impossible, eg only allowing cigarettes to be sold on one day of the year, then the restriction would be caught by Article 30. To White and also Steiner 29 (1992) CML Rev 749 the Sunday Trading cases should not fall within Article 30 at all, not even as justified exceptions. Wyatt & Dashwood also submit that Article 30 has no application where indistinctly applicable measures affect the volume of sales of imports and domestic products alike.

There are signs that the ECJ is now following this approach. The case of *Keck and Mithouard* (1993) signals a retreat from the severity of the *Dassonville* formula. The applicants had been prosecuted for reselling goods at below cost price which was contrary to French law. The ECJ held that Article 30 does not apply to national legislation imposing a general prohibition on resale at a loss. Applying the *Dassonville* formula the court found that the measures would restrict the volume of imports but that regard should also be had to the purpose behind the legislation and the 'rule of reason'. The court said that provided the measures apply (1) to all traders operating in the Member State and (2) the marketing of domestic and imported goods are affected in the same manner (both in law and in fact) then Article 30 does not apply. The extent of the ECJ's re-appraisal of Article 30 will become apparent from further caselaw. Steiner in *Textbook on EC law* (4th ed) submits that *Keck* is a modification but not an abandonment of the rule of reason. She argues that a measure which operates as a hindrance to imports in fact as well as in law, will require justification under the rule of reason.

Article 34 – exports

Article 34 prohibits quantitative restrictions on exports. Obviously these are less restrictive than quantitative restrictions on imports.

There is less likely to be a danger of protectionism so the ECJ takes a more lenient view of them.

The *Dassonville* test does not apply to exports. Consequently, export measures which are indistinctly applicable do not come within Article 34. Measures have to be overtly or covertly protectionist by having, as their object, the restriction of export trade, in order to provide an advantage for national production or for the domestic market of the State in question at the expense of the production or of the trade of the other Member State. The thinking behind Article 34 is that if exports are prohibited then the national market will be flooded with domestic production easing out competition from other Member States.

Indistinctly applicable measures

Where restrictions apply equally to domestic products for export and domestic products for the national market there is no breach of Article 34. So in *PB Groenveld BV* (1979) a ban on the possession of horse meat by manufacturers of meat products was not intended to create an advantage for the product in the national market and did not come within Article 34. The court rejected the approach of Advocate General Capotorti who had applied the *Dassonville* and *Cassis* tests.

Similarly, in *Oebel* (1981) a restriction on night working and delivery hours for bakery products restricted both exports and goods intended for the domestic market and consequently did not breach Article 34.

Distinctly applicable measures

A quality inspection and export licences for watches breached Article 34 in *Bouhelier* (1977) as no such inspection or licence was required for watches which were being sold on the domestic market.

Again in *Jongeneel Kass BV v Netherlands* (1984) a rule requiring inspection documents for exports breached Article 34 as it was not required for goods to be sold on the domestic market.

Exceptions to the principle of free movement

There are several classes of exemption to the prohibitions in Articles 30 and 34 on quantitative restrictions and measures having equivalent effect. The most important exceptions are contained in Articles 36 and 115. The exceptions in Article 36 differ from those in *Cassis de Dijon* as they apply to both distinctly and indistinctly applicable measures and they are an exhaustive list which cannot be added to in the way the 'mandatory requirements' have been supplemented.

Article 36

Article 36 provides that Articles 30-34 shall not preclude prohibitions or restrictions on imports, exports or goods in transit justified on the grounds of public morality, public policy or public security; the protection of health and life of humans, animals or plants; the protection of national treasures possessing artistic, historic or archaeological value; or to the protection of industrial and commercial property.

These exceptions are subject to three restrictions. First, they cannot constitute a means of arbitrary discrimination between Member States, so are subject to the general principle of proportionality. Secondly, they must not constitute a disguised restriction on trade between Member States. As they are exceptions to the right to free movement they are to be interpreted strictly. Thirdly, where the Community has passed harmonising legislation then the Member States cannot impose any more stringent restriction on goods.

Public morality

The question of public morality first arose in *R v Henn and Darby* (1979). There were different Scottish and English provisions relating to the import of pornographic material, so a special set of rules were applied to imports. It was argued that the rules were discriminatory, as they were applied specifically to imports. However, there was no lawful domestic trade in such literature in the UK. It was held that as effective measures were taken to prevent the domestic trade, there did not have to be identical provisions applied to imports.

If there are no effective measures taken to prevent domestic trade, then imports cannot be prohibited on grounds of public morality (*Conegate v HM Customs and Excise* (1986)). The UK prevented the importation of life size inflatable female dolls but there was no prohibition on manufacturing or marketing such objects in the UK so the ban could not come within Article 36.

Public security

The public security exception was successfully argued in *Campus Oil* (1984). Importers into Ireland were forced to buy petrol from Ireland's only refinery. Ireland argued that it needed a refinery for strategic reasons. It was held that purely economic objectives could not justify an exception under Article 36 but if a measure could be justified on other grounds such as the maintenance of essential supplies it would not be excluded from Article 36 even though this might also serve economic purposes.

The exception was subject to certain restrictions. Firstly, the purchasing obligation could be imposed only if no less restrictive measure was capable of achieving the same object. Secondly, the quantities covered by the scheme could not exceed the minimum needed to ensure the security of the State.

The protection of the health and life of humans, animals or plants

Restrictions for the protection of public health and life of humans, animals and plants must satisfy three conditions:

- it must not be a disguised form of discrimination;
- the degree of regulation must be proportionate;
- a real health risk must be proved (*Duphar v Netherlands* (1984)).

In *De Peijper* (1976) certain information had to be supplied to relevant authorities before pharmaceuticals could be marketed in the Netherlands. The product in question was virtually identical to a product which had already been marketed in the Netherlands and the information had already been disclosed with respect to these products. Restrictive measures were, therefore, not necessary in this case.

Inspections

An inspection may be justified in the event that imported plants constitute a real risk which is not present in analogous domestic products (*Rewe-Zentralfinanz GmbH v Landwirtschaftskammer* (San Jose scale) (1975)). German law imposed an inspection on imported products where none existed on domestic products. The court examined the purpose of the inspections, which was to control San Jose scale and was therefore justified. The court said:

... the different treatment of imported and domestic products, based on the need to prevent the spread of a harmful organism could not be regarded as arbitrary discrimination if effective measures are taken in order to prevent the distribution of contaminated domestic products, and there is a risk of the harmful organism's spreading if no inspection is held on importation.

So discriminatory treatment can be justifiable under this heading but only if effective measures serving the same purpose are taken with regard to the equivalent domestic product. Such discriminatory measures would include bans, tests and inspections to ensure domestic standards are met and licensing or documentary requirements to prove this fact.

So in *Commission v UK* (UHT) the UK could protect the health of consumers by a requirement that importers produce certificates issued by the competent authorities of the exporting Member States, coupled with controls by samples.

Health certificates

Member States may only make spot checks on goods coming from another Member State when they are accompanied by health certificates from the State of origin *(Commission v Italy* (1993)).

Additives

Additives have caused problems where they have been permitted in some Member States but not others. In *Commission v Germany* (1988) there was a blanket prohibition by Germany on all additives in beer. The court said, insofar as scientific opinion is uncertain and there is an absence of harmonisation, it was for Member States to decide the degree of protection. If goods containing an additive are approved in one Member State and imported into another Member State the importing Member State must:

- authorise the use of the additive if scientific committees showed it to be harmless to individuals and it meets a technical need;
- make readily available to companies an administrative procedure for seeking a general authorisation for use of the additives, authorisation procedure must be concluded reasonably quickly;
- ensure an action is brought before the courts with respect to a refusal to grant an authorisation.

The court ruled that Germany had not satisfied these conditions and so the legislation was not justified.

The protection of national treasures possessing artistic, historic or archaeological value

The case of *Commission v Italy* (art treasures) (1968) involved a restriction on art treasures which took the form of an export tax. It was held that Article 36 could not be relied on to justify a tax. Although there was some *obiter dicta* to support the view that a quantitative restriction would have been legal.

Industrial and commercial property

Protection of industrial and commercial property comes within the permitted derogations, this section looks at its effect on free movement

116

of goods although it is an area which also has implications for the competition law and harmonisation of laws.

Existence and exercise/specific subject matter

Article 222 of the Treaty provides that:

The Treaty shall in no way prejudice the rules in Member States governing the system of property ownership.

This rule means that the existence of industrial property rights remain unaffected by the Treaty but their exercise can, in certain cases, be a contravention of Community law. Community law will only protect industrial property rights insofar as the exercise of the right is a protection of its specific subject matter. The specific subject matter of the right can be taken as the right to be the first to market the product but only with the right holder's consent. Any further attempts to enforce the right are not permissible as the rights will be 'exhausted'. The ECJ has been concerned to prevent the 'partitioning' of markets ie to stop the exercise of industrial property rights leading to the re-erection of national barriers to trade and therefore impeding the integration of the internal market.

The distinction between the existence and the exercise of rights has created concern as it has been said by the ECJ that Article 30 is not addressed to undertakings but to Member States. This emphasis on the exercise of rights was thought to bring private undertakings within Article 30. However, the favoured view is that the source of rights is national legislation which determine the circumstances in which parties can exercise their rights and national courts are simply applying these provisions.

The exhaustion of rights principle

The case of *Deutsche Grammophon v Metro* (1970) was a notable first for applying Articles 30 to 36 to industrial property rights independently of the Treaty provisions on competition.

Deutsche Grammophon had manufactured certain records in Germany which were sold to its subsidiary Polydor in Paris and then came into the hands of Metro. Deutsche Grammophon sought an injunction against Metro selling the records in Germany, in contravention of its rights under German law, which roughly equated to the British concept of copyright.

The ECJ said that the Treaty did not prevent the existence of such industrial property rights as copyright but the exercise of the rights could fall within the terms of the Treaty. Article 36 only permits derogations to the extent that they are justified to safeguard rights constituting the specific subject matter of the property.

The right could not be relied on to prevent the re-importation of the product into the Member State where it was first marketed as this would isolate the national market and would be contrary to a single market. The specific subject matter of the right was to protect Deutsche Grammaphon's right to have the records marketed for the first time only with their consent. The rights are exhausted when a product has been lawfully distributed on the market of a Member State by the owner of the right or with his consent.

Patents

The exhaustion of rights principle applies to patents (*Merck v Stephar* (1981)). Pharmaceuticals were patented in the Netherlands but it was not possible to patent them in Italy. The defendant acquired quantities of the product on the Italian market and attempted to export them to the Netherlands. It was held following *Deutsche Grammaphon* that once goods had been marketed with the holder of the patent's consent then the rights had been exhausted and could not be relied on.

The same principle was adopted in *Centrafarm BV v Sterling Drug Inc* (1974). Pharmaceuticals were 50% more expensive in the Netherlands than in the UK. The plaintiff bought in the UK and sold in the Netherlands. The patent in both countries was held by the licensee. Again a derogation from Article 30 was not permitted as the product had been put in the market in a lawful manner with the patent holder's consent.

This can be contrasted with the situation where the product has been marketed without the patent holder's consent, in which case there can be an enforcement of the rights. In *Pharmon v. Hoechst* (1985), Hoechst had a patent for manufacturing a certain medicine in both the UK and the Netherlands.

In 1972 DDSA Pharmaceuticals Ltd, obtained a compulsory licence from the UK Patent Office to exploit the invention. The UK Patent Office was obliged to grant this licence unless there were 'good reasons' for refusing. Under the terms of the licence DDSA were prohibited from exporting the product. DDSA disregarded this prohibition and exported to the Netherlands by selling the medicine to Pharmon. The parties arguments revolved around whether Hoechst could be regarded as having exhausted their rights under the patent. It was held that where a Member State has granted a compulsory licence which allows marketing and manufacturing operations to be carried out which could normally be prevented by the patentee, the patentee cannot be deemed to have allowed the marketing and the rights can be enforced.

Trademarks

The Trademarks Directive was passed in 1989 with the aim of approximating aspects of trade mark law which affect the functioning of the common market, to ensure that the conditions for obtaining and holding a trade mark are the same in the Member States.

Centrafarm v Winthrop (1974) arose out of the same facts as *Sterling Drug* but this case related to the trademark, Negram. The same principles relating to exhaustion of rights as have been used in copyright and patents were applied to trademarks. Consequently, a trademark which was owned by the UK and Dutch subsidiaries could not be used to prohibit the sale of a product which the firm had marketed itself under the trademark in another Member State with the firm's consent.

Re-packaging

The thinking was developed further in *Hoffman-La Roche v Centrafarm* (1978). In this case the problem of re-packaging was addressed. Centrafarm acquired valium tablets on the British market where they had been marketed by the plaintiff. Centrafarm re-packaged the tablets and affixed the plaintiff's trade mark before selling them on the German market.

The court said that a trademark was a guarantee to the consumer that a product had not been interfered with by a third party without authorisation. However, a prevention of marketing re-packaged products would be a disguised restriction on trade within Article 36 if the following criteria could be satisfied:-

* repackaging could not affect the product;
* the proprietor receives prior notice of the marketing of the product;
* it states on the product who has done the re-packaging.

Objective justification

In *Centrafarm BV v American Home Products Corpn* (1978), the ECJ held that it would not be possible to use different trademarks in different member states unless there was an 'objective justification' for doing so.

Objective test

The test for determining whether there is a disguised restriction on trade within Article 36 is an objective not a subjective test (*Pfizer v Eurim-Pharm* (1981)). It simply has to be proved that the rights have been exercised in such a way that there had been a partitioning of the common market not that it was intended to partition the common market.

Copyright

In *Musik-Vetrieb Membran v GEMA* (1981) records which had been marketed in the UK were imported into Germany. There was a difference in the royalty fees, 6.5% was paid in the UK and 8% was payable under German law. The principle of exhaustion applied and the additional royalties could not be claimed. With regard to the subject matter of the right, it had been argued that the exhaustion principle did not apply to copyright as it was to enable the author to claim ownership of the work and to object to any distortion of the work. The court said copyright included those rights but it also comprised other rights such as the right to commercially exploit the work.

Partitioning of national markets was allowed in *Coditel v Cine Vog Films* (1982). The plaintiffs had exclusive rights to show the film *Le Boucher* in Belgium, the defendants were broadcasting the film from Germany into Belgium. The plaintiffs were allowed to enforce their rights and prevent the German transmissions. It should be noted that this is not a free movement of goods case but a services case. It is significant as the court suggested that performing rights were different to literary rights – the principle of exhaustion did not apply in the same way and rights could be enforceable in one Member State.

A fee for video lending rights is a permitted derogation under Article 36 (*Warner Bros v Christiansen* (1988)). Renting of videos can be distinguished from classic copyright as it is of a continuous nature. The restrictions involved applied equally to imported products and domestic products alike.

A Directive providing for the harmonisation of copyright and related rights has been adopted by the Council.

Common origin

The ECJ developed the doctrine of 'common origin' in *Van Zuylen Frères v Hag* (1974). A German company acquired the Hag trademark in Belgium and Luxembourg in 1908. Later a Belgian subsidiary was formed and the trademark was transferred to it. At the end of the war the shares in the subsidiary were seized by the Belgian government and sold. The German and Belgian trademarks were of common origin but were not held by different parties.

It was held that the exclusiveness of a trademark right could not be relied on against a product lawfully produced in another Member State where the competing trademark had a common origin.

Rejection of the 'common origin' doctrine
The court abandoned the doctrine of 'common origin' and effectively reversed its earlier decision in *CNL-SUCAL NV v Hag GF AG (Hag 2)* (1990). The court found in *Hag 2* that the element of consent was lacking in applying the 'exhaustion of rights principle', therefore, the trademark could be relied on.

Articles 30 to 36 only apply to restrictions on trade between Member States. In *EMI v CBS* (1976) the ECJ held that exhausted rights could be relied on where the goods were being imported into the EC from the US.

Arbitrary discrimination

The most obvious form of arbitrary discrimination is against imports in favour of domestic products either by applying a restriction to imported products or by applying a greater restriction with respect to imported products.

In *Commission v France* (1980) advertising restrictions on alcoholic drinks fell more heavily on grain based spirits than on fruit based spirits. It was claimed that the restrictions were justified on the ground of public health, the measures could not be so justified as they constituted a disguised restriction on trade as France produced fruit based spirits and grain based spirits were imported from other Member States.

'Disguised restriction'

The case of *Commission v UK* (Newcastle poultry disease) (1982) concerned a ban on imports into the UK of poultry products, eggs and egg products from those Member States (including France) which did not have a policy of slaughtering foods infected with Newcastle disease. The UK sought to justify the ban on animal health grounds but the court found that the real purpose was to protect domestic production.

The ECJ had taken into account that there had been pressure for a ban from UK turkey producers. The ban had been introduced hastily and also when French producers had attempted to comply with the new restrictions an additional requirement had been introduced.

Article 115

In addition to Article 36, a second derogation from the free movement of goods rules is provided by Article 115. This Article is designed to prevent deflection of trade. It entitles the Commission, in certain circumstances, to authorise a Member State to take protective measures against goods imported from a third country but currently in free circulation in another Member State.

Revision Notes

Introduction to free movement of goods

- Treaty provisions on Free Movement of Goods Articles 3, 12-17, 30-36 (goods), 38-43 (agriculture);
- furtherance of Community objectives Article 3 (a), 3(b);
- Single European Act 1986 Articles 8(a) (now Article 7(a)), 100(a);
- Treaty establishing European Economic Area;
- position under amendments made under the Treaty on European Union.

Customs Union (Article 9)

Consists of two parts:

Free trade area consisting of a group of territories where duties have been eliminated and a common tariff adopted in trade relations with the outside world.

(a) Common Customs Tariff (CCT) Articles 18-29

'Free circulation' of goods once CCT paid.
   Member States cannot unilaterally impose charges in excess of the CCT (*Diamantarbeiders v Indiamex*) (1973).
   Member States can charge for health inspections where these are allowed in internal Community trade (*Simmenthal v Italian Finance Administration*) (1978).
   Article 30 (elimination of quantitative restrictions and measures having equivalent effect) applies to goods in 'free circulation' (*Donckerwolke* (1976), *Tezi v Commission* (1986)).

(b)   Common Commercial Policy (CCP)
Derogation from free movement before commercial policy is completed (Article 115).

Scope of the provisions of free movement

The meaning of 'goods'
Includes goods which have a 'monetary value and constitute the object of commercial transactions': *Commission v Italy* (1968) 'art treasures

case' (1968); goods in 'free circulation' (*Commission v Ireland* (Cyprus potatoes) (1985)) case.

Does not include television broadcasts *Debauve* (1980); coins which are a 'means of payment' (*R v Thompson*) (1978).

Who is bound?

* Community;
* Member States, including 'organs' of the State and private bodies receiving government sponsorship *Commission v Ireland* ('Buy Irish'); privatised government utility (*Foster v British Gas*);
* do not have horizontal direct effect (*Officier van Justitie v Van de Haar* (1984)); (*Apple and Pear Development Council v Lewis* (1983)).

Customs duties and charges having equivalent effect

* Customs duties and charges having equivalent effect are eliminated (Articles 12-17).
* 'Genuine' taxes fall outside Articles 12-16 and come within Article 95. Definition of 'genuine' tax can be seen in *Commission v France* 'reprographic machines' (1981).
* Member States can make the following charges on imports provided they fulfil the following criteria:

(a) Charges for services rendered, provided the charge is related to the service ((*Ford España v Spain* (1989)); charges for customs formalities must be outside mandatory opening hours (*Commission v Italy* (1987) (customs hours) and charge must be proportionate to service (*Commission v Italy* (1993) (Extraordinary Customs Clearance)).

(b) Charges relating to requirements of Community law, charges for inspections only allowed where inspections are mandatory either under Community law as in *Bauhuis* or international conventions (*Commission v Netherlands* (1977)).

Internal taxation Article 95

Imports can be subject to internal taxation provided that the system does not discriminate between imports and domestic products or similar products.

* Articles 12-15 and Article 95 are mutually exclusive.
* Similar domestic products include those that meet the same needs (*Commission v France* (Taxation of Spirits) (1980)) and goods which

may compete in the future (*Commission v UK* (excise duty on wine) (1980)).
- Taxation of imports permitted where there is no similar competing domestic product as in *Fink- Frucht* (1986).
- Discriminatory taxation of imports permitted where the difference in treatment is due to objective reasons of government policy (*Vinal v Orbat* (1981)).

Quantitative restrictions and measures having equivalent effect Article 30

- No *de minimis* rule (*Van de Haar* (1986))
- Definition of quantitative restriction (*Geddo v Ente Nazionale Risi* (1973))
- Commission's interpretation of Article 30: Directive 70/50. Distinction between 'distinctly applicable' measures which apply only to imports and 'indistinctly applicable' measures which apply to imports and domestic products alike.
- ECJ's interpretation of Article 30 can be seen in *Dassonville* (1974). A much wider definition of measures having equivalent effect than the Commission's to include 'indistinctly applicable' measures.
- Modification of the scope of the *Dassonville* formula in *Cassis de Dijon* (1979). 'Indistinctly applicable' measures are justified or fall outside Article 30 if they come within the 'rule of reason'. Member States can impose their own laws on imports where they satisfy certain 'mandatory requirements'.
- Conditions for coming within the 'rule of reason':
  - (a)   'indistinctly applicable' measure;
  - (b)   no harmonisation of safety legislation under Article 100(a);
  - (c)   'mandatory requirements' relating to:
    - (i)   fiscal supervision;
    - (ii)   fair competition;
    - (iii)   public health;
    - (iv)   consumer protection and (added by later cases);
    - (v)   issues of social policy;
    - (vi)   environment;
    - (vii) cultural issues.

- Article 30 does not apply to national legislation imposing a general prohibition on resale at a loss (*Keck and Mithouard*) (1993).
- Inconsistency of the ECJ's approach. Sometimes the ECJ has treated trading rules as falling outside Article 30 *Blesgen* (1982), *Quietlynn*

(1990) and on other occasions has treated matters as being within Article 30 but justified under the 'rule of reason' as in the Sunday Trading cases. More recently the ECJ signalled the start of a reduction in the scope of the *Dassonville* formula taking measures outside the ambit of Article 30:

(a) where legislation not intended to regulate intra-Community trade;
(b) measures apply to all traders operating in the Member State;
(c) the marketing of domestic and imported products are affected;
(d) in the same manner (both in law and in fact) (*Keck*).

Exports – Article 34

Article 34 prohibits restrictions on exports. However, the rules are far less reaching than for imports and measures are only caught if there is a difference in treatment for exports as opposed to goods meant for the domestic market (*Bouhelier* (1977), *Jongeneel Kass* (1984)).

Exceptions to free movement

Article 36

Article 36 provides for a number of exceptions to the free movement principle but there are restrictions on the extent to which they can be invoked:

- cannot constitute a means of arbitrary discrimination, so are subject to proportionality;
- must not be a disguised restriction on trade;
- cannot be invoked where harmonising legislation exists;
- cannot be invoked to justify a purely economic objective (*Campus Oil* (1984)).

Public morality

Restrictions on imports do not have to be identical to those on domestic products (*R v Henn and Darby* (1979)). Must be restrictions on domestic products as in *Conegate*.

Public security

If the primary purpose of the measure is to protect public security it can be invoked even if the measure coincidentally fulfils an economic objective (*Campus Oil* (1984)).

Protection of health

This cannot be invoked if it is system of disguised discrimination and regulations must satisfy proportionality. Inspections are justified where measures are taken to stop spread of organisms (*Rewe - Zentralfinanz GmbH* (San Jose scale (1975)). Must be a real threat to health (*Duphar* (1984)).

Industrial and commercial property

The existence of industrial property rights is allowed but their exercise is restricted (*Deutsche Grammaphon* (1970)). EC law will only permit the exercise of the rights to the extent that it protects the specific subject matter of the right. Once a product has been marketed with the right holder's consent then the rights are exhausted and cannot be relied on to prevent imports.

Article 115

The Commission can authorise Member States to take protective measures against goods from a third, country, which are in 'free circulation' to prevent deflections from trade.

5 Competition law

Aims of competition law

The aims and objectives of competition law are varied and changeable. They include a mixture of political and economic aims and can sometimes conflict. They will respond to changing patterns of trade, with emphasis being governed by prevailing conditions.

Integration

Competition law clearly aids the creation of a common market as it reinforces the provisions of the Treaty aiming at the removal of barriers between the economies. There would be little value in removing barriers to trade if undertakings could replace them with their own restrictions, such as an agreement not to trade in each other's territory. This would re-create market divisions on national lines.

Consumer protection

Competition law has a role in protecting consumers against price fixing, excessive charges and unfair trading conditions on the part of undertakings. It also ensures that consumers receive a fair benefit of any restrictive agreement.

Efficiency

If an undertaking is able to exercise monopoly power over prices it will be able to raise its prices above cost (which for these purposes includes normal profit). This is regarded as inefficient as there will not be the best allocation of resources with consumer demands not being satisfied. There is a further waste of resources on the part of the undertaking in acquiring its monopoly power over prices.

It is felt that competition encourages firms to improve their performance relative to their competitors. It also has an innovative function, by encouraging the introduction of new products.

Fair competition

The preamble to the Treaty refers to 'fair competition'. This covers such aspects as the prohibition of subsidies by national governments, the application of competition rules to non EC companies which are trading within the Community, a fair balance between the public and private sector and the protection of small and medium enterprises. The latter concern ensures that there is a healthy market structure and that smaller firms are not swallowed up by larger firms.

It is sometimes difficult to reconcile 'fairness' with the other aims of 'efficiency' and 'integration'. Snyder in *New Directions in Community Law* identified two different perspectives as to what competition law was attempting to achieve. Using the sheepmeat market regime as an example, he found that the UK emphasised the free trade aspects of competition law, which is consistent with the market in the UK being integrated into the global economy.

By contrast, the French market was not integrated into the global economy. Instead, the marketing chain was involved in local production; the market faced a sudden disturbance with large quantities of imports from the UK. Whereas the British saw competition policy being concerned with free trade and trade policy, the French saw it more in terms of market structure and structural policy and as a method of protecting their smaller producers from the effects of sudden competition from larger foreign producers.

Jurisdiction of the competition rules

Extra territorial application

Article 85 applies to arrangements between undertakings 'which may affect trade between Member States and which have, as their object or effect the prevention, restriction or distortion of competition within the common market' and Article 86 applies to any abuse of a dominant position 'within the common market or in a substantial part of it ... in so far as it may affect trade between Member States'.

Undertakings which are carrying on business in the Community can therefore enter into agreements that affect competition in third countries provided the performance of those agreements takes place entirely outside the common market.

Undertakings which are outside the common market can still be caught by the provisions of competition law.

Doctrine of enterprise entity
Action has been taken against a parent company which is situated outside the Community where it has a subsidiary within the Community and the commercial policy is controlled by the parent company. In this situation the subsidiary's actions are imputed to the parent company. This occurred in *ICI v Commission 'Dyestuffs'* (1972), before the UK's accession to the Community.

It is also clear from *Instituto Chemicoterapico Italiano and Commercial Solvents v Commission 'Commercial Solvents'* (1974) that the ECJ will readily infer that the parent company exercises control over the subsidiary.

Parallel application of competition rules

National legislation relating to competition is hardly affected by the existence of Community competition law. Undertakings are expected to comply with both systems except to the extent that enforcement of national provisions would affect the uniformity of Community law. In *Walt Wilhelm* (1972) it was said by the ECJ that:

Should it prove that a decision of a national authority regarding an agreement would be incompatible with a decision adopted by the Commission ... the national authority is required to take proper account of the effects of the latter decision.

From this it would seem that national authorities should not take action under national rules against agreements which have been exempted under Community law.

Article 85

For Article 85(1) to apply three elements must exist:

- collusion between undertakings;
- which must affect trade between Member States;
- which has as its object or effect the distortion of competition within the common market.

Collusion between undertakings

The collusion may take at least three forms:

- agreements between undertakings;
- decisions by associations of undertakings;
- concerted practices.

Agreements between undertakings

Agreement

The concept of an agreement is wider than a contract. So it has been held to include a 'gentleman's agreement' (*ACF Chemiefarma v Commission* (1970)). It included an unsigned agreement in *BP Kempi* (1979), as the agreement had been implemented by the parties.

'Agreement' can also include unilateral conduct. In *AEG-Telefunken v Commission* (1983) AEG prohibited resale of its goods except to dealers who had been 'approved'. AEG argued that its refusal to admit dealers to its dealership network was a unilateral act and could not therefore be an agreement. It was held by the court that 'refusals of approval are acts performed in the context of the contractual relations with authorised distributors' and therefore came within the definition of 'agreement'. The ECJ said that there was a 'tacit' acceptance by other distributors of the exclusion when they entered into agreement with AEG.

This concept of 'tacit acceptance' was again used in *Sandoz Prodotti Farmaceutici SpA v Commission* (1990). Invoices were stamped 'export prohibited' and this was held to be an agreement as when distributors settled their accounts on the basis of these invoices there was a 'tacit acceptance' of Sandoz's act, even if the distributor did not abide by the term.

Undertaking

The test for an undertaking is whether the natural or legal person is carrying on a commercial or economic activity. The test is therefore a broad one and includes a company, partnership, sole trader and association.

It includes a public undertaking, with pre-privatised British Telecom being held to come within Article 85 in *Italy v Commission* (1985). It has been held to include an inventor in *Reuter/BASF* (1976) and opera singer in *Re Unitel* (1978). The liberal professions were once thought to be outside the definition of undertaking but given these decisions that is now doubted.

The conduct of a subsidiary company is imputed to its parent, at least where the subsidiary is following the parent's instructions (*Instituto Chemicoterapico Italiano and Commercial Solvents v Commission* (1974)). If a subsidiary company disobeys its parents instructions then the parent is not responsible and it is the subsidiary that should be fined *(BMW Belgium v Commission* (1979)).

An agreement between a parent and a subsidiary falls outside Article 85 where it relates to 'distribution of tasks' amongst the group (*Centrafarm v Winthrop* (1974)).

An agreement between a former parent and its privatised subsidiary comes within Article 85 (*Austin Rover and Unipart* (1980)).

A group of companies controlled by the same person is treated as one undertaking (*Hydrotherm v Andreoli* (1974)).

An agency agreement where the agent acts purely for the principal and takes no part in the risks of a transaction falls outside Article 85 (*Suiker Unie* (1975)).

Decisions by associations of undertakings

This catches decisions of trade associations. The ECJ has not been concerned with the legal status of these associations so it is immaterial whether the association enjoys legal personality or not. In a federal trade association all the members consist of other trade associations, nevertheless these were held as coming within Article 85 in *BNIC v Clair* (1985).

'Decisions' includes not only binding decisions but also non binding recommendations (*Vereeniging van Cementhandelaren v Commission* (1972)).

Concerted practices

This aspect of Article 85 is aimed at price fixing by cartels. It also ensures that Article 85 catches practices for which there may be no contractual arrangement and yet are able to inhibit competition, in this sense it performs a 'mopping up' role.

Concerted practices were defined in *ICI v Commission* (1972) as:

A form of co-ordination between undertakings which, without having reached the stage where an agreement properly so called has been concluded, knowingly substitutes practical co-operation between them for the risks of competition.

In *Suiker Unie* it was argued that a concerted practice required a plan between producers. The ECJ held that there did not have to be an actual plan as such. Each producer must have independently adapted to market conditions.

[The requirement of independence] does strictly preclude any direct or indirect contact between such operators, the object or effect of whereof is either to influence the conduct on the market of an actual or potential competitor or to disclose to such a competitor the course of conduct which they themselves have decided to adopt or contemplate adopting.

Particular problems arise with oligopolies. An oligopoly exists where there are a few dominant firms in a market. In a classic oligopoly there is an homogeneous product and it is difficult for new producers to enter into the market. The difficulty is that companies in an oligopoly have to respond to changes in their competitor's prices. There will be no price fixing agreement as such, the undertakings are simply responding to market conditions. An example of an oligopoly is petrol companies who tend to have very similar price movements.

In *ICI v Commission 'Dyestuffs'* it was accepted that what superficially may appear to be price fixing can be oligopolistic interdependence but it was also said that the burden of proof would be on the defendant to show that there was collusion.

The Court defined what has become known as 'conscious parallelism':

Although parallel behaviour may not by itself be identified with a concerted practice, it may however amount to strong evidence of such a practice if it leads to conditions of competition which do not correspond to the normal conditions of the market.

In the *Dyestuffs* case there was found to be concertation on the basis that the producers had met; some of the characteristics of an oligopoly were found not to exist and there was circumstantial evidence that there was concertation.

For there to be concertation there must be 'contact' between undertakings. Attendance at a meeting where information was disclosed was held to be 'contact' in the *Polypropylene* cases.

Advance notice of price rises can be amount to a concerted practice. There can be sound commercial reasons for announcing price rises in advance but in *Allstrom v Commission (Woodpulp)* (1988) the system of quarterly price quotations was considered to be concerted practice as it allowed for information about prices to be spread amongst producers.

Evidence of concerted practice

It can be extremely difficult to prove a concerted practice. Parallel behaviour can be arrived at independently of other undertakings by traders simply taking sensible decisions about the market; identical movements in price can simply be a response to a competitor's action. 'Contact' is a wide concept which goes beyond the concept of agreement and can include passive activities such as attending meetings and advance notices of price changes which could be for commercial reasons.

There has been concern expressed by academic writers such as Korah in *EEC Competition Law and Practice* that too little weight will be placed by the Commission on commercial reasons for parallel behaviour. It is felt that the Commission, in the *PVC* and *LdPE* (1989) decisions, too easily inferred a concerted practice. In the *Dyestuffs* decisions, which includes *ICI V Commission* greater reliance seems to have been placed on the circumstantial evidence than on the direct evidence of meetings between the producers. In the *Woodpulp* decision, the judgment seems uncertain as to whether intention to participate in a concerted practice is required before an advance notice can be regarded as 'contact'.

Despite this it has been held that parallel behaviour can have an objective basis. In *SACEM* (1989) copyright collection societies outside France refused to grant licences to discotheques in France. It was argued that it would be onerous for the authorities to negotiate and check these licenses and it was held that it should not be presumed that there was a concertation where there was another objective reason for the behaviour.

Similarly, objective reasons for behaviour were found in *CRAM and Rheinezink v Commission* (1984) two zinc producers were found to have stopped deliveries of zinc to a Belgian producer shortly after it had been discovered that the dealer was making parallel imports of the zinc into Germany, rather than re-exporting them to Egypt as had been agreed in the contract. It was held that there had been imprecise evidence of a concerted practice as there had been difficulties in receiving payment which could also have accounted for the parallelism.

The Commission has said that concertation can be proved by:

Economic analysis showing that under the given circumstances the similarity of prices was economically inexplicable unless there was concertation beforehand.

This statement has not satisfied academic writers that producers will not be punished when the parallelism has arisen for commercial reasons.

Affecting trade between Member States

Article 85(1) only applies where there is an agreement 'which affects trade between Member States'. The purpose of this rule is to set the boundaries for the jurisdiction of national law and Community law. If there is no effect on inter-State trade then national competition rules will apply. The question of whether an agreement affects trade between Member States can be approached in more than one way.

Usually it will be determined by the effect of an agreement on the flow of goods and services between Member States. It was said in *Société Technique Minière v Maschinenbau Ulm* (1966):

For this requirement to be fulfilled it must be possible to foresee with a sufficient degree of probability on the basis of a set of objective factors of law or of fact that the agreement in question may have an influence, direct or indirect, actual or potential, on the pattern of trade between Member States.

Another method is where 'the structure of competition within the common market [is affected]' as in *Hulin v Commission* (1979).

A third method was suggested by Advocate General Trabucci in *Groupement des Fabricants de Papiers Peints de Belgique v Commission* (1975) when he said that it must 'affect the attainment of the objectives for which the common market was established'.

The first two methods refer to the integration of the common market and are aimed at the prevention of the erection of barriers around national markets, whereas the third is wider and includes all the Community's objectives.

Increase in trade

Where there is a deflection of trade it does not matter that the effect of the agreement has been to increase trade.

In *Consten and Grundig v Commission* (1966), there was an agreement between Consten and Grundig that Consten would be Grundig's exclusive dealer in France. Consten were allowed to register Grundig's trademark in France. The French market was isolated as dealers in other countries were not allowed to sell their goods in France. A third party acquired Grundig's goods in Germany and began selling them in France. Consten sued for infringement of its trademark. It was held that the agreement infringed Article 85, even though there had been an increase in trade as a result of the agreement. The agreement had led to a partitioning of the market so it was immaterial that it had led to an increase in trade.

Indirect effect on trade

In *BNIC v Clair* (1985) the agreement concerned a raw material that was not usually exported. Although this, in itself, did not affect inter-State trade, products in which the raw material was incorporated were exported, and so the agreement came within Article 85 as it had an indirect effect on trade.

Agreements affecting the whole of a territory

In *Cementhandelaren v Commission* (1972) it was said:

An agreement extending over the whole of a territory of a Member State by its very nature has the effect of reinforcing the compartmentalization of markets on a national basis thereby holding up the economic interpenetration which the Treaty was designed to bring about ...

An agreement between parties in one Member State, where the agreement only relates to activities within that State, can have an indirect effect on trade as it leads to the partitioning of national markets.

Effect on a parent company

In *Verband der Sachversicherer eV v Commission 'Fire Insurance'* (1987) German law provided that insurance co.npanies from other Member States doing business in Germany had to have a branch office situated there. A recommendation of a trade association as to minimum fire premiums was held to effect trade between Member States as it affected the financial relationship between the branch office and the foreign head office.

Look at whole agreement

It was held in *Windsurfing v Commission* (1986) that it was necessary to look at the whole agreement. If the whole agreement affects trade between Member States then it is irrelevant that individual restrictions do not affect trade.

Trade must be affected to an appreciable extent

Article 85(1) is subject to a *de minimis* rule. Trade must be affected to an 'appreciable' extent. In *Völk v Vervaecke* (1969) Völk had granted an exclusive distribution deal in Belgium and Luxembourg. Normally, this would have been regarded as a partitioning of the market but as Völk produced less than 1% of the washing machines in Germany, the agreement did not have an appreciable effect on trade.

The Commission have issued guidance in their Notice on Minor Agreements. In the Commission's view trade between the Member States will not be affected to an appreciable extent if:

- the goods or services which are the subject of the agreement do *not* represent more than 5% of the total market for such goods;
- the aggregate turnover of the undertakings involved does not exceed 200 million ECU.

Both Advocate General Warner (*Schallplatten Miller v Commission* (1978)) and Advocate General Dutheillet de Lamothe (*Cadillon v Hoss* (1971)); (*Béguelin Import v GL Import-Export*) have said that the ECJ is not bound by the Commission's notice. Of course, the ECJ itself has accepted a *de minimis* principle in the *Völk* case but it is possible that an agreement could come within the Commission's notice and yet still be found to breach Article 85(1) by the ECJ.

Network agreements fall outside the Commission's notice, as it says:

Where in a relevant market competition is restricted by the cumulative effects of parallel networks of similar agreements established by several manufacturers or dealers.

Small firms are likely to be part of a network and therefore this provision deprives the notice of much of its effectiveness. The ECJ has said in *Holleran v Thwaites* (1989) that where a manufacturer has entered into a network of agreements the approach is not to look at one agreement but to look at them all to decide whether there has been an appreciable effect on trade. The Court of First Instance in *Delimitis* (1991) has said that where an agreement is part of a network it is necessary to see if it significantly adds to the foreclosing of a market.

Object or effect the distortion of competition

Object

In *Consten and Grundig v Commission* it was held that the 'object' of the agreement had been to restrict trade as it lead to market sharing and also because of the exclusivity of the agreement whereby Consten would only handle Grundig's products and Grundig would not supply anyone else in France.

The words 'object' and 'effect' were found to be disjunctive by the ECJ if the object was found to be anti-competitive then it was not necessary to show that the effect was to restrict competition. In this case Consten and Grundig had argued that the effect had been to increase trade but this was found to be irrelevant. It was also held that if the object was to restrict competition then it was not necessary for there to be a market analysis.

Consten and Grundig is also significant as it makes clear that Article 85 applies to 'vertical' as well as 'horizontal' agreements. A 'vertical' agreement is an agreement between a producer and distributors, while a 'horizontal' agreement is an agreement between producers. The latter are clearly anti-competitive as it is an arrangement between competitors. The ECJ's willingness to include 'vertical' agreements has been criticised, as it is argued by American economists that they increase competitiveness because they enable producers to compete more effectively by improving their wholesale and retail network. Wyatt and Dashwood, in *European Community Law* (3rd ed), argue that this reasoning does not necessarily apply in the European Community where the law is attempting to integrate the market and there is a need to guard against partitioning national markets which exclusive distribution agreements can facilitate.

Effect

When considering the 'effect' of an agreement it was held in *Sociéte Technique Minière v Ulm* (1966) that it is necessary to have a market analysis. The following considerations should be taken into account:

- the nature or quantity of the goods or services involved;
- the market share and turnover of the parties;
- the effect on parallel importers;
- is the market oligopolistic?
- what are the barriers to entry?

Rule of reason

If an agreement does not have, as its object, the restriction of competition then the consequences of the agreement should be considered taking the legal and economic consequences into account to see if the effect is to prevent, restrict or distort competition. Agreements of both a vertical and horizontal nature are caught by Article 85(1). Where the aim is not to restrict competition then a 'rule of reason' approach is used. As the aim of the agreement is not to restrict competition the offending clauses are examined to see if they are necessary to achieve the aim of the agreement. The rule of reason requires a balancing between the restrictive effects of the agreement and the benefits to be gained from it.

The rule of reason has been shown to allow a degree of protection against competition in a number of different ways.

First, where the protection is an 'indispensable inducement' to finding a business partner. In *Sociéte Technique Minière v Maschinenbau Ulm* an exclusive distribution agreement was necessary to extend activities into another Member State. This furthers the integrative aim of competition law by facilitating access to new markets within the common market.

Protection against competition was necessary in *Nungesser v Commission* (1982) where a new item was being introduced onto the market. This can be contrasted with *Pronuptia de Paris v Schillgalis* (1986) where an exclusivity provision came within Article 85(1) as the trademark was well known and there could be no novelty value.

Secondly, the rule of reason has been held to apply where the restrictive provisions are necessary to allow a distribution franchising system to work properly (*Pronuptia*). Franchising is where an entrepreneur develops a winning formula with regard to a trademark, product, shop layout or selling style and in return for a lump sum and/or royalties, franchises his knowledge to franchisees who wish to join into the network without having to spend resources developing the system themselves. The ECJ accepted that restraints on competition would be necessary to make a franchising system work. However, the court held that the granting of an exclusive territory together with an obligation to sell only from a franchised outlet would confer absolute territorial protection and therefore infringe Article 85(1) when the network was widespread. The Commission has since adopted Regulation 4087/88, which provides block exemption for certain franchises.

The third area where the rule of reason has been held to apply is where a selective distribution network has been established on the basis of objective qualitative criteria. For high quality or high technology goods it may be necessary for a producer to ensure that distributors are of a high quality to ensure that they give the appropriate sales advice and right level of after sales service. Selective distribution will mean that goods are more expensive but against this, gains in the level of service provided can be offset. The ECJ has accepted in *Metro v Commission (No 1)* (1977) and *AEG v Commission* (1983) that when selective distribution is done on qualitative grounds then it is outside Article 85(1). However, when it is done on a quantitative basis it does come within Article 85(1).

Although the Commission and the ECJ have been moving towards a rule of reason, neither has acknowledged the rule as such. In order to increase legal certainty, the Commission's preferred approach has been to issue Notices indicating types of agreement which are acceptable under Article 85(1) and introducing block exemptions for certain types of agreement. The Commission have issued a Notice on Co-operation between National Courts and the Commission in applying Articles 85 and 86, to give national courts assistance when deciding whether an agreement falls within Article 85(1).

State measures which institute anti-competitive behaviour

Articles 85 and 86 are addressed to undertakings and not to Member States. Restrictive practices are often dependent, for their effectiveness, on government action which reinforce agreements which promote concerted practices.

The ECJ have to an extent circumvented these problems through use of a combination of Articles 3(g); 5 and 85.

Article 3(g) provides for 'the institution of a system ensuring that competition in the common market is not distorted'.

Article 5(2) provides that Member States are required to 'abstain from any measure which could jeopardise the attainment of objectives of the Treaty'; the Court said in *Leclerc v Au Blé Vert Sàrl* (1985) that this put Member States under an obligation not to detract from the application or effectiveness of Community law or to allow legislative measures which render the competition rules ineffective.

Government encouragement is no defence/mitigation to Article 85

In *BNIC v Clair* a trade association had government backing. The trade association made a recommendation as to price to its members contrary to Article 85. It was no defence that the association had government backing.

State/measures reinforcing anti-competitive agreements

In *BNIC v Aubert* (1987) a ministerial order extended the recommended price of the trade association and made it binding on non-members. Using a combination of Articles 3(g), 5(2) and 85 the ECJ held that this was illegal and that Community law took priority.

State measures which leave the fixing of prices to citizens

In *Leclerc v Au Ble Vert Sàrl* a French law required publishers and importers of books to fix minimum retail prices for books. Retailers were only allowed to discount these prices by a maximum of 5%. A resale maintenance price agreement would have been contrary to Article 85 if it had been concluded amongst the undertakings themselves however, in this case the combination of Articles 3(g), 5(2) and 85 were too general and blunt an instrument to prevent the national measures from being held contrary to Community law. The provisions relating to importers were found contrary to the free movement of goods provisions but they are provisions addressed to the Member States.

In *Cullet v Leclerc* (1985) the French government itself fixed the minimum prices for petrol and again it was held that Article 85 had not been deprived of its effectiveness.

Effect of infringement

Article 85(2)

Article 85(2) declares that all agreements, decisions and concerted practices caught by Article 85(1) shall be absolutely void, although there is the possibility of exemption under Article 85(3). The entire agreement may be unenforceable or it may be possible to sever individual provisions and leave the rest of the agreement intact. There is no Community-wide principle of severance, so the mechanism for determining severance is left to the Member State. This has been criticised by Whish in *Competition Law* (3rd Ed) as depriving Community law of uniform effect. In English courts the method adopted is the 'blue pencil' test.

Exemptions

Exemptions can only be granted by the Commission and cannot be granted by national courts. This puts national courts in a difficult position, as they are required to apply Article 85(1) but they are unable to grant exemptions.

The Commission's Notice on Co-operation (1993) is designed to help national courts. The Notice allows national courts to consider and apply 'substantive provisions of individual exemptions' and comfort letters. These are 'factual elements' the national court takes into account in deciding whether Article 85 applies. If the national court is still unable to make a decision it may apply to the Commission for the following information: whether the agreement has been notified; whether a decision has been issued or comfort letter sent; when a comfort letter is likely to be sent; an interim opinion on whether the agreement is likely to obtain negative clearance or exemption. However, a decision of the national court is still capable of challenge.

Exemptions will be granted in situations where there are restrictive aspects to the agreement but there are also beneficial effects. These beneficial effects may achieve other aims of the Community and the function of Article 85(3) is to balance effective competition with the Community's other tasks.

Agreements can be excepted in one of two ways:

- individually, by decisions adopted by the Commission;
- under a block or group exemption.

Individual exemption

The Commission's sole power to grant exemptions causes difficulties as it has insufficient resources to deal speedily with all the applications it receives for individual exemption, so delays are encountered. In order to take advantage of Article 85(3) agreements must be notified to the Commission on Form A/B. The Commission can give negative clearance, which is a formal decision that Article 85(1) does not apply to the agreement or it can grant exemption, ie Article 85(1) does apply to the agreement but it is to be exempted. The Commission only grants formal decisions exempting agreements in 'priority' cases due to its lack of resources. In most cases, the Commission sends a 'comfort letter' whereby it indicates that it intends to close its file and would have been minded to grant individual exemption or negative clearance had it continued with the case.

As the Commission has a monopoly over the grant of individual exemptions it acts as a 'repeat player' and can adopt its own policy towards various types of agreement over a period of time. Whish contends that as Article 85(3) is a flexible provision conferring a wide discretion it is better to measure an agreement against the Commission's policy objectives rather than the criteria laid down in Article 85(3). The Commission is also able to negotiate with parties before issuing a decision and get clauses it dislikes removed and impose terms and conditions. In this sense agreements become a 'negotiated compromise' between the parties and the Commission.

The Commission's priority has been to favour exemptions which promote collaboration between small and medium sized undertakings. More recently, it has been favouring collaboration between larger firms. This is probably a reflection of the need for size to compete in increasingly globalised markets and to meet the challenge of American and Japanese competition.

The four requirements of Article 85(3)

Article 85(3) lays down four conditions which must be satisfied before exemption can be granted. All four conditions must be satisfied, two of these conditions are positive and two are negative.

The two positive conditions are:

- that the agreement must contribute to improving the production or distribution of goods or to promoting technical or economic progress;
- that the agreement allows consumers a fair share of the resulting benefit.

The two 'negative' conditions are:

- that the agreement does not impose upon the undertakings concerned restrictions which are not indispensable to the attainment of these objectives;
- the agreement does not afford the undertakings the possibility of eliminating competition in respect of a substantial part of the products in question.

Benefit

The 'benefit' produced by the agreement must outweigh its disadvantages. Improvements in production have been found to flow from specialisation agreements and research and development. Specialisation agreements enable parties to achieve economies of scale. Research and development avoids duplication and enables parties to reach findings more quickly.

Patent and know how licensing agreements and manufacturing joint processes enable inventions and processes to be exploited more widely. A shift in recent times can be detected in favour of these agreements. As mentioned at the beginning of the chapter competition law is a fluid instrument and whereas at one time a patent licensing system was treated with suspicion, with the rise of new technologies they are seen as a way of rewarding invention. Similarly, joint venture agreements may have been, at one time, viewed as a way of dominating the European market but with the increasing globalisation of markets, are now seen as a way of competing effectively with Japanese and American competitors.

Globalisation has also seen exemption being granted to exclusive dealership networks where they help to penetrate world markets. They can lead to benefits in production where there is an exchange of information between the manufacturer and distributor, they can also lead to improvements in distribution. Other types of arrangement which have lead to an improvement in distribution include a selected dealers' network and rationalisation of participation in trade fairs.

As well as taking into account economic benefits which have been derived from agreements the court has also taken into account social benefits. The Commission has therefore looked kindly towards 'crises cartels' where companies have sought to come together and tried to mitigate the harsher effects of competition during recession or long term decline in an industry. Such an exemption was granted in *Re Synthetic Fibres* (1985) where demand had not kept up with increases in output and the agreement was aimed at reducing over capacity.

Employment is another objective the Commission has said it takes into account. Cushioning the effects of decline in an industry provides the opportunity of minimising the effects on employment by affording time to retrain workers. It is disputed whether the Commission is allowed to take these social considerations into account but Whish argues that Article 85 should be interpreted teleologically so that it is read in the light of Articles 2 and 3, which allows these wider objectives to be taken considered.

Fair share to consumers

'Consumer' does not necessarily mean members of the public who purchase for private use. It will also include undertakings who purchase the goods in the course of their trade. Improvements in production and/or distribution are thought to be of benefit to consumers as they will receive a better or cheaper product. There is no definition of fair share but where the intensity of competition is great in the market then consumers are considered likely to receive a fair share of the benefit.

No indispensable restrictions

Clauses seeking absolute territorial protection are usually considered dispensable although they have been frequently allowed in exclusive distribution agreements and intellectual property licenses.

The Commission use this criteria to have provisions of agreements they are unhappy with removed. This has been seen by Korah and Wyatt & Dashwood as compelling parties to renegotiate agreements after they have been concluded. This is not seen as necessarily beneficial to the European economy as it may deter high technology firms from establishing themselves here as they may not want their agreements to be re-opened.

No substantial elimination of competition

This is the least considered of the criteria either because an agreement has failed under one of the other heads or because it has been considered too beneficial when considering the other heads to fail here.

Usually agreements between firms with a large market share will be considered as eliminating competition but some have been allowed, particularly when European firms have been faced with intense competition from Japanese or American firms.

The Commission have to define the relevant product market. What products can be considered as substitutes for the product in question? In *Kali und Salz AG v Commission* (1975) a decision against refusal to exempt an agreement was annulled as the product market had not been properly defined.

The Commission must also define the geographical market. Sometimes competition will have been substantially eliminated if it has been significantly reduced in one Member State; sometimes it will have to have been reduced in the common market as a whole and sometimes it will have to have been reduced globally.

Operation of agreement in practice

In *Re Ford Werke AG Agreement (No 2)* (1983) the Commission refused to exempt an agreement when it did not object to any of its terms but to how it would be implemented in practice. Ford refused to supply right hand drive cars to its German distributors. The purpose of this provision was to help Ford of Britain. The price of cars in the UK was substantially higher and Ford was attempting to stop imports from Germany to the UK to keep the UK market sealed.

Block exemptions

Article 85(3) provides for categories of agreement to be granted exemption. Consequently, the Commission, acting under powers granted to it by the Council, can grant block exemptions. These have the dual advantage of removing uncertainty from businesses and reducing the Commission's workload.

It is usually easier to draft an agreement so that it comes within a block exemption rather than notify an agreement and apply for an individual exemption. In this way block exemptions can be said to be imposing 'model' agreements. Regulations have now been passed which provide for block exemptions.

White clauses
Each regulation contains 'white' clauses which are clauses which are restrictive of competition but are eligible for block exemption.

Black clauses
These are clauses which if included will make the agreement ineligible for exemption.

Grey clauses
These are clauses which do not usually come within Article 85(1) but which are listed for certainty.

Opposition procedure
This is an infrequently used method of obtaining individual exemption. An agreement which is outside the block exemption is notified to the Commission and if the Commission does not express its opposition within six months the agreement is exempt.

Regulations granting block exemptions have been passed in the following categories:

- Exclusive Distribution Regulation 1983/83. This provides for exclusive distribution but absolute territorial protection will take the agreement outside the terms of the exemption. It only covers agreements between two undertakings but network agreements are also thought to be covered. It only covers goods which are 'for resale'.
- Exclusive Purchasing Regulation 1984/83. This can be beneficial as it can streamline competition but it can also keep other potential competitors out of the market. Competing manufacturers and 'tying' agreements are excluded. There are special provisions for the brewery industry and petrol 'solus' agreements.
- Patent Licensing Regulation 2349/84. Where a patentee grants a licence to use the patent for the consideration of royalties.
- Specialisation Regulation 417/85. Where two parties agree to concentrate in future on certain product lines and to cross supply each other with the products which they are specialising.
- Research and Development Regulation 418/85.
- Motor Vehicles Regulation 123/85.
- Franchising Regulation 4087/88. Only applies to distribution franchises, not to wholesale or manufacturing franchise.
- Know how Licensing Regulation 556/89.

Article 86

Abuse of a dominant position

Article 86 provides that:

Any abuse by one or more undertakings of a dominant position within the common market or in a substantial part of it shall be prohibited as incompatible with the common market in so far as it may affect trade between Member States.

Dominance

The treaty does not define a dominant position. It was defined by the ECJ in *United Brands Co v Commission* (1978) as:

A position of economic strength enjoyed by an undertaking which enables it to prevent competition being maintained on the relevant market by giving it the power to behave to an appreciable extent independently of its competitors, customers, and ultimately of its consumers.

The Commission has added a further element in *AKZO v Commission* (1986):

The power to exclude competition ... may also involve the ability to eliminate or seriously weaken existing competition or to prevent potential competitors from entering the market.

Before it is possible to determine whether an undertaking is dominant it is necessary to analyse the relevant market. The relevant market has to be analysed from three perspectives: the product market, the geographical market and the temporal market.

Relevant product market

This revolves around the substitutability of the product. It is often necessary to look wider than the product itself. If a producer raises prices consumers may be able to switch to a similar product in which case there is 'cross elasticity of demand'. Alternatively, a rival supplier may be able to adapt existing products or provide suitable substitutes for consumers in which case there will be 'cross elasticity of supply'.

Cross elasticity of demand

The leading case is *United Brands*. The Commission argued that the relevant product market was bananas. The applicants argued that a rise in the price of bananas would lead consumers to switch to other fruits, therefore the relevant product market should be fruits. The ECJ found that the relevant market was bananas. They found only a small amount of evidence for cross elasticity of demand and found that there was a significant market that were unable to switch to alternative hard fruits such as the old, elderly and infirm.

This tends to overlook situations where consumers are 'locked in' to using a particular product. In such situations the consumers will be unable to switch demand to another product.

An example is spare parts. Once a consumer has decided to buy a particular product then the choice of spare parts may be limited to those made by the manufacturer of the original product. In *Hulin* (1979) the ECJ found that the relevant market for spare parts for Hulin cash registers were not interchangeable with parts for other cash machines and so consumers were entirely dependent on Hulin for supplies. The relevant market was that for Hulin spare parts even though they only had a very small share of the market for cash registers.

The relevant market may also be narrowed by the existence of sub-markets. For example, in *ITP v Commission* (1991) it was accepted by the CFI, that the market for television programme information could be divided into markets for weekly programme listings and magazines in which they were published.

In *Brass Band Instruments Ltd v Boosey & Hawkes plc* (1988) Boosey and Hawkes had themselves identified British brass bands as a market separate from the market for brass instruments in general which lead to the adoption of a narrow market definition.

Cross elasticity of supply

In *Europemballage Corp and Continental Can v Commission* (1973) an American company, through its German subsidiary, held a dominant position in the German market for light metal containers for meat products, light metal containers for fish products and metal closures for glass containers. The Commission had considered the cross elasticity of demand as it had considered the extent to which meat and fish suppliers could use plastic and glass containers. The ECJ annulled the Commission's decision and said that supply substitutability should also have been considered. Existing suppliers of, for example, tins for vegetables might have easily been able to adapt their production processes to compete if Continental Can had raised its prices unduly.

Structure of supply and demand

It is sometimes necessary to look at market structure when looking at interchangeability. In *Nederlandsche Banden-Industrie Michelin v*

Commission (1983) the replacement tyre market for heavy vehicles was found to be a separate market from the tyre market for new vehicles. Even though they were identical products they would be demanded and supplied in very different circumstances.

Raw materials can form a separate market from an end product
In *Commercial Solvents* (1974) the applicants had refused to supply a firm called Zoja with a raw material which was used in the production of a drug. The applicants contended that the relevant market was the wider market for the drug not the narrower market for the raw material where there dominance could be easily proved. This was rejected by the court which held that the raw material could be a market in its own right.

Relevant geographical market
The ECJ requires that the geographical market be defined. In deciding whether a firm has market power the geographical context has to be taken into account. The relevant geographical market is defined by Steiner in *Textbook on EC Law* as 'the market in which available and acceptable substitutes exist'. Transport is a primary consideration. If goods are easily and cheaply transported around the Community then the geographical market will be drawn widely. Consumer tastes can also affect the geographical size of a market, as can the homogeneity of a product. The geographical size of a market can therefore be part of a State, a Member State or the Community as a whole.

In *Michelin* it was held that the Commission had been correct in taking the Netherlands as the relevant market. A French company had been conducting business through its Dutch subsidiary but its competitors were also using local subsidiaries and therefore that was the level competition was conducted on, as the conditions of competition were the same.

In *United Brands* it was held that the Commission were right to exclude three of the nine Member States (as they were then) from the relevant market as conditions for importing and marketing were different in those three States.

Guidance on the relevant geographical market has been provided by the Commission's notice on agreements of minor importance.

Article 86 is subject to a *de minimis* rule as it provides that there must be a 'dominant position within the common market or a substantial part of it'. The 'substantial part' is not to be assessed on a geographical basis but in terms of the economic importance of the area as defined.

In *Suiker Unie* it was said:

... the pattern and volume of the production and consumption of the said product as well as the habits and economic opportunities of vendors and purchasers must be considered.

In *Suiker Unie* the size of the Belgium and South German sugar markets were taken in relation to the size of the Community sugar industry as a whole.

Advocate General Warner in *BP v Commission* (1978) said that reliance should not be placed on percentages alone in determining a substantial part.

A criticism made of the approach to a relevant geographical market is that it fails to take into account the position of third countries. An undertaking may be dominant in the area of the Community but may face substantial competition world-wide.

The temporal market
In assessing the relevant market it is necessary to consider the temporal aspects. Competitive conditions can vary through the year as substitute products become available or as consumer habits vary. It has been argued that in *United Brands* the Commission should have taken into account that in the summer greater competition existed when bananas compete with summer fruits.

In *ABG Oil* (1977) the temporal effects of the oil crises of the early 1970s were taken into account. Oil companies were under a duty to treat their customers fairly during the crises. They were in a dominant position during the years 1973-74 as oil was not available from other sources.

This view has been challenged by Advocate General Warner in *BP v Commission* as in his view short term crises do not give freedom of action, as there is the risk of desertion once the crisis has ended.

Market power
Once the relevant market has been determined it is necessary to work out whether the undertaking is actually dominant within it. This is done by reference to a number of criteria.

Market share
The greater the market share the greater the likelihood of dominance. In *Commercial Solvents* there was virtually a 100% market share. In *Continental Can* the share was 70-80%.

Market structure
Market shares can be much lower than this such as 45% share of *United Brands*. The *United Brands* case is interesting because it was thought to be dominant even though it faced tough competition. The market share was retained despite the liveliness of the competition which pointed to independence of action. In addition to absolute share it is also necessary to look at relative size. If an undertaking is much bigger than its nearest competitor, then a smaller market share will suffice. The Commission has said that a 20-40% market share can constitute dominance.

Other factors
Market share is only one factor that is taken into account in assessing dominance. If there are few barriers to entry in an industry then a large market share would quickly see the emergence of competitors which is indicative of there ever having been market power.

Barriers to entry
There is debate amongst economists as to what constitutes a barrier to entry. The Chicago School in the US takes a minimalist view. It sees a dominant position as encouragement to new undertakings to enter the market and as a result the market will correct any imbalances. The European market is far less integrated than the US and a less relaxed view of barriers to entry is taken in Community law.

Financial resources
Access to large financial resources enables an undertaking to enjoy freedom of action. In *Continental Can* emphasis was placed on the access to the financial capital markets.

Vertical integration and distribution systems
The greater control over vertical integration, the greater the ability to act independently of the competition. An example is *United Brands* which had an advantage in respect of privileged access to supplies, means of transport and distribution outlets.

Brand loyalty
Sometimes the accumulative effect of a protracted advertising campaign is to make consumers loyal to a particular brand and consequently insensitive as to the merits of competing brands. It requires extensive resources to overcome this sort of loyalty with rival campaigns.

Conduct and performance

A firm's conduct can be taken as evidence that it is dominant. Conduct can be defined as activities pursued by an undertaking in the course of a business eg prices, sales promotion etc whereas performance is the result of these activities eg profits. Wyatt and Dashwood contend that conduct in itself is not sufficient evidence of dominance.

In *United Brands* two conflicting performance criteria had to be taken into account. United Brands had been losing money over several years which indicated a lack of dominance, whereas it had retained its market share; greater weight was given to the latter.

Length of time

According to economic theory if perfect competition exists then when an undertaking achieves a dominant position and accrues above normal profits, this will be a green light for competitors to enter the market. Therefore, dominance has to be maintained over a period of time before it can be demonstrated that the market is not working properly.

Technological resources

Superior technological resources will enable a firm to keep ahead of its rivals.

Collective dominant position

Article 86 refers to 'abuse by one or more undertakings' of a dominant position.

Oligopolies

In *Hoffman-La Roche v Commission* (1979) the ECJ rejected the possibility of oligopolies jointly enjoying a dominant position. Agreements between monopolies would have to be caught by Article 85 and not by Article 86.

The Commission have been keen to establish the idea of joint collective dominance. In the *Italian Flat Glass* (1989) they issued a decision in which they claimed that an oligopoly had been jointly abusing its position. Together the companies had enjoyed independence from competition.

On appeal to the CFI the court rejected the idea that the companies had been jointly dominant as the Commission had not considered the relevant product, geographical and temporal markets but it accepted (*obiter*) that an oligopoly could be jointly dominant.

Subsidiaries

Legally distinct enterprises are considered one undertaking if they are subject to the same control. So in *Continental Can* the effect of three companies were taken into account: Continental Can (the American parent); SLW (a German subsidiary) and Europembellage (also a subsidiary) in determining dominance. Similarly, in *Commercial Solvents* the American parent and its Italian subsidiary were both looked at in assessing dominance.

Abuse

A dominant position is not in itself illegal, there must also have been an abuse of the position. Although dominance is not in itself actionable, it does bring special responsibilities. It was said in *Michelin* that a firm in a dominant position 'has a special responsibility not to allow its conduct to impair competition'.

Article 86 itself refers to exploitative behaviour where an undertaking deals harshly with consumers through, for example, charging high prices or tying agreements.

There is no definition of 'abuse' in the Treaty and Article 86 has been interpreted teleologically, in particular against the objectives established by Article 2 and 3(g). This has ensured that exclusionary anticompetitive abuses have been brought within Article 86. Since *Continental Can* it has been clear that where a dominant firm reduces competition in a market then that is also abusive behaviour. Examples of exclusionary behaviour include a refusal to supply, predatory pricing and acquisition of competitors.

It is clear from the *Hoffman-La Roche* case that 'abuse' is an objective concept, so there is no need to show that the undertaking intended to cause harm. So 'abuse' may exist in the absence of intention but it may also exist in the absence of fault. In *Continental Can* the applicant was trying to take over a rival firm and it argued that there was no evidence that it would drive the target out of the company should its bid prove unsuccessful. The applicant had therefore done nothing wrong. It was held to be an abuse for a dominant firm to strengthen its position and significantly reduce competition by taking over a rival.

Behaviour which is *prima facie* abusive may be legal if it is objectively justified. Although behaviour may be anti competitive that may not be the object behind it. If behaviour is objectively justified then the undertaking must have behaved proportionately. In other words the behaviour must not exceed that which is necessary in order for it to achieve its objective.

Anti-Competitive abuses

Mergers
Continental Can and *Warner-Lambert/Gillette* (1993) are both cases where Article 86 has been used to prevent mergers. A Regulation has now been adopted for the control of mergers.

Predatory pricing
An undertaking may price its goods low in order to drive potential competitors from the market. In *AKZO* (1985) predatory pricing was found to occur when the applicant cut its prices in order to keep a competitor out of the market. The Court held that where 'prices [are] lower than the average variable costs ... must be regarded as an abuse'.

Refusal to supply
In *Commercial Solvents* refusal to supply raw materials to an existing customer with the intention of driving it from business was held to be an abuse.

Similarly, in *Boosley & Hawkes* attempts by the applicant's distributor to market their own brass instruments led to the applicant cutting off supplies and engaged in harassing tactics in order to frustrate their competitor's fledgeling business.

Refusals to supply a new customer have been held to constitute abuse.

Other cases have included refusals to supply spare parts as in *Hulin* and refusal to grant copyright licenses as in the *TV listings* cases.

The Commission is also developing an 'essential facilities' doctrine under which a dominant undertaking which owns and controls a facility must give equal access to it to competitors (*Sealink/B and I - Holyhead (interim measures)* (1992)).

Rebates
A distinction is made between loyalty discounts which are caught by Article 86 and quantity discounts which are not. A loyalty discount is a reduction in price granted on condition that a specific proportion of the buyer's requirements are bought from the supplier. Loyalty discounts were condemned in *Hoffman-La Roche* as was the system of buyers notifying Hoffman-La Roche if they received more favourable prices from other manufacturers, enabling Hoffman to consider whether they would match the price or allow the buyer to buy elsewhere without loss of rebate. The choice of freedom of supplies was still left in the hands of Hoffman-La Roche.

Target discounts were condemned in *Michelin* whereby dealers received a discount on achieving a certain target. It was felt to limit dealers choice of supplier, as they would concentrate on obtaining their discount.

Tying

Tying is where a condition of entering into a contract is that supplementary obligations are entered into as well. This can be seen in *Hilti* (1992) where buyers of nail cartridges were required to buy nails as well.

Excessive prices

In *United Brands* and *General Motors Continental v Commission* (1975) high prices which '[have] no reasonable relation to the economic value of the product supplied', were condemned.

Exclusivity

In *Tetra Pak* (1990) an abuse occurred where a firm acquired a company which had an exclusive licence for a competing technology.

Enforcement of Articles 85 and 85

Regulation 17

The Commission has been given a wide variety of powers to deal with infringements of competition law. The most important piece of legislation being Regulation 17/62.

Proceedings for the application of Article 85 or Article 86 may be started by the Commission on its own initiative or as a result of an application for negative clearance and/or notification of an agreement for an individual exemption or as a result of someone laying a complaint.

However, in the latter case, the Commission has stated in its Notice on Co-operation (1993) that complainants should look to protect their directly effective rights before national courts and not by laying complaints.

Fact finding

Article 11

Article 11 enables the Commission to request from the governments and competent authorities of Member States and undertakings and associations of undertakings 'all necessary information'.

There is a two stage procedure. First, the Commission asks for specified information by a given date. There is no obligation to comply with the request but fines can be imposed for misleading information.

Secondly, if the information is not forthcoming then the second formal stage is entered into whereby the Commission adopts a decision ordering that the information be supplied. Failure to comply with this decision can result in the imposition of fines or penalty payments.

Article 14

Article 14 empowers the Commission to carry out investigations to ensure compliance with competition rules.

The Commission can enter premises of undertakings, to examine and take copies of, or extracts from books and business records and to ask for oral explanations on the spot. No advance notice need be given of investigations.

Voluntary investigation

Under Article 14(2) the Commission is authorised in writing to carry out an investigation. The undertaking may refuse but if it agrees it must co-operate fully. The written authorisation must set out the subject matter and purpose of the investigation and the penalties for incomplete investigation. Failure to co-operate fully can lead to a fine.

Mandatory investigation

The Commission may adopt a decision requiring an undertaking to submit to an investigation. The Commission is required first to consult with national authorities. This provision has been used as the basis of 'dawn raids' on the undertaking and the Commission can demand that the investigation be carried out immediately. Failure to comply with the investigation can lead to fines or penalty payments.

The decision must set out the subject matter and purpose of the investigation.

Privilege

The Commission cannot see documents which are protected by lawyer/client privilege (*AM & S v Commission* (1982)). Privilege is subject to conditions:

* the document must be made in the client's defence;
* privilege does not extend to in house lawyers;
* it does not extend to lawyers not practising in the EU.

Professional secrecy

Article 20 provides that the Commission shall 'not disclose information acquired as a result of this Regulation and of the kind covered by the obligation of professional secrecy.' In *Adams v Commission* (1985) it was held that there is an obligation to protect the identity of informants.

Privilege against self incrimination
It has been held in relation to Article 11 that there is a privilege against self incrimination (*Orkem v Commission* (1989); and *Solvay v Commission* (1989)). This would probably apply under Article 14 but it is limited because it only extends to refusing to answer incriminating questions, companies can be compelled to hand over documents which are incriminating.

Decisions

Negative clearance
This is certification that neither Articles 85 or 86 apply to the case. Application is made on Form A/B and the Commission must publish its decision. Negative clearance will not be binding on a national court which can apply stricter provisions of national law. Negative clearances can also be dealt with informally.

Individual exemptions
Only the Commission can grant individual exemption. In practice very few individual exemptions are granted and they tend to be used strategically in areas where the Commission is developing its policy.

Block exemptions
The Commission may confirm that the agreement comes within a block exemption or there may be an opposition procedure contained in the block exemption.

Comfort letters
The Commission has insufficient resources to deal with all the cases which have been notified to it and has endeavoured to bring cases to an end informally. The Commission will often enter into negotiations with the parties trying to get them to change terms of the agreement; it may then state that it is closing its file. Both negative clearances and individual exemptions can be dealt with in this way.

Comfort letters are not binding on national courts. 'Formal' comfort letters are where details of the agreement are published to give third parties an opportunity to object. 'Informal' comfort letters involve no publicity.

Infringement proceedings

Before it can enforce Article 85 or 86 the Commission is obliged under Article 19 of the Regulation to give the parties the opportunity to be heard. If Regulation 17 does not apply it was held in *Transocean Marine Paint v Commission* (1974) that there is a general principle of *audi alterem partem*.

Statement of objections

Where infringement proceedings are being brought a statement of objections must be served on the undertaking. The statement cannot take action in respect of any matter that is not dealt with in the statement of objections. It will not normally be possible to obtain judicial review of a statement of objections.

The respondent will be invited to make its views on the statement of objections known within a specified period. It will also be told that it can apply for an oral hearing.

Final decision

Order to terminate infringement
The Commission can order parties to refrain from further infringements. In *Commercial Solvents* supplies were ordered to be resumed to a customer. However, it was held that it is not possible to order supplies under Article 85 but only under Article 86 (*Automec v Commission (No 2)* (1992)).

Fines
The Commission can fine up to 1 million ECUs or 10% of turnover in all products world-wide, whichever is the greater.

Interim measures

Regulation 17 is silent on the question of interim relief but the ECJ has held in *Camera Care v Commission* (1980) that there is the power to grant interim relief. The right is subject to four conditions:

- the case is urgent;
- measures are needed to to avoid a situation likely to cause serious and irreparable damage to the party seeking them;
- measures are of a temporary or conservatory nature;
- measures are restricted to what is necessary.

In adopting decisions implementing interim decisions parties are entitled to a hearing and the decision must be in a form that is capable of challenge.

Serious and irreparable harm

It was held in *La Cinq v Commission* (1992) the CFI held that the Commission was wrong to look for serious and flagrant breaches of the competition rules before granting interim measures. The Commission should have asked itself whether the situation was capable of being remedied by a final decision. In this case there was the possibility of La Cinq going out of business if it was not granted interim measures.

This recent decision only sparingly could increase the amount of interim measures which have hitherto been granted.

Temporary and conservatory nature

The measures must be of a temporary and conservatory nature. The Commission cannot therefore grant a temporary order where it would not have the same power to grant a final order (*Ford v Commission* (1985)).

Undertakings

Interim measures will not be granted if undertakings can be obtained from the parties instead.

Judicial review by the court

The Commission's decisions are controlled by way of judicial review by the Court of First Instance and by appeal on points of law to the European Court of Justice.

The following rights of action may apply:

- Article 175: Failure to Act;
- Article 173: Action for Annulment;
- Article 172: Penalties;
- Interim measures: decisions for interim measures must be in a form capable of judicial review.

Revision Notes

Aims of competition law

The following have been identified as aims of competition law, although it should be noted that the aims are variable and changeable:

- integration;
- consumer protection;
- efficiency;
- fair competition.

Jurisdiction of the competition rules

Article 85 applies to arrangements between undertakings which may affect trade between Member States or prevent, restrict or distort competition within the common market.

Article 86 applies to any abuse of a dominant position within the common market or a substantial part of it in so far as it affects trade between Member States.

The following rules will apply:

- undertakings situated within the Community will not be caught if agreements take place entirely outside the community;
- undertakings outside the Community are caught by the rules if a subsidiary is acting within the Community (*Dyestuffs* (1972));
- the ECJ readily find that a parent company exercises control over the subsidiary (*Commercial Solvents* (1974)).

Article 85

For Article 85(1) to apply three elements must exist:

- collusion between undertakings;
- which affect trade between Member States;
- which has its object or effect the distortion of competition.

Collusion between undertakings

These can take three forms:

- agreements between undertakings;
- decisions by associations of undertakings;
- concerted practices.

Agreements between undertakings

Agreement

This has been given a wide definition and includes:

- a 'gentleman's agreement' (*ACF Chemiefarma* (1970);
- an unsigned agreement (*BP Kempi* (1979);
- unilateral conduct (*AEG-Telefunken* (1983), *Sandoz* (1990)).

Undertaking

The test for an undertaking is whether a natural or legal person is carrying on a commercial or economic activity.

The test is a broad one and has been held to include:

- public undertaking (*Italy v Commission* (1985));
- an inventor (*Reuter/BASF* (1976));
- an opera singer (*Re Unitel* (1978)).

Decisions by associations of undertakings

This includes:

- federal trade associations (*BNIC v Clair* (1985));
- non-binding recommendations (*Cementhandelaren* (1972)).

Concerted practices

This is aimed at price fixing by cartels and arrangements which fall short of a contractual arrangement.

Concerted practices have been defined as:

'A form of co-ordination ... which ... knowingly substitutes practical co-operation ... for the risks of competition' (*Dyestuffs* (1972)).

Oligopolies

There are particular problems in deciding whether oligopolies are engaging in a concerted practice or are responding to market conditions.

The ECJ defined what has become known as 'conscious parallelism':

'... parallel behaviour may not by itself be identified with a concerted practice, it may amount to strong evidence ... if it leads to conditions ... which do not correspond to the normal [market] conditions' (*Dyestuffs* (1972)).

Affecting trade between Member States

The agreement must affect trade between Member States. The following rules have been found to apply:

- the agreement can still affect trade between Member States even though it has increased trade between them (*Consten and Grundig* (1966));
- it includes an indirect effect on trade (*BNIC v Clair* (1985));
- agreements which affect the whole of a territory of one Member State are included (*Cementhandelaren* (1972));
- a recommendation which effects the relationship between a parent company and a subsidiary, affects trade between Member States (*Fire Insurance* case (1987));
- it is necessary to look at the whole agreement (*Windsurfing* (1986));
- trade must be affected to an appreciable extent, ie there is a *de minimis* rule (*Völk* (1969), Commission's Notice on Minor Agreements).

Object or effect the distortion of competition

Object
The words 'object' and 'effect' are disjunctive. Consequently, in *Consten and Grundig* where it was shown that the object of the agreement was anti-competitive, it did not matter that the effect was pro-competitive.

Effect
When considering the 'effect' it is necessary to have a 'market analysis' (*Sociéte Technique Minière v Ulm* (1966)).

Rule of reason
Where an agreement has a pro-competitive object but an anti-competitive effect, then the rule of reason may operate to take the agreement out of Article 85(1). Offending clauses will first be examined to see if they are necessary to achieve the aim of the agreement. The rule of reason has allowed the following:

- restrictive agreements which are an 'indispensable inducement' to finding a business partner (*Sociéte Technique Minière* v Ulm);
- protection against competition where a new product is brought onto the market (*Nungesser* (1982));
- restrictive provisions necessary to allow a franchising agreement to work properly (*Pronuptia* (1986));
- a selective distribution agreement which is established on the basis of qualitative criteria (*Metro (No 1)* (1977), (*AEG* (1983)).

State measures which institute anti-competitive behaviour

The competition rules are primarily addressed to individuals but it has been held that they can affect Member States through a combination of the effect of Articles 3(g), 5 and 85.

Effect of infringement

The entire agreement may be unenforceable or it may be possible to sever individual provisions and leave the rest intact. The mechanism for determining severance is left to the Member State.

Exemptions

Agreements can be excepted in one of two ways:

- individually, by decisions adopted by the Commission;
- under a block or group exemption.

Individual exemptions

Article 85(3) lays down four conditions which must be satisfied before exemption is granted to an agreement:

- it must contribute to improving production or distribution of goods or to promoting technical or economic progress;
- allows consumers a fair share of the resulting benefit;
- does not impose restrictions which are not indispensable to the attainment of the objectives;
- does not afford the possibility of eliminating competition in respect of a substantial part of the product in question.

Block exemptions

The Commission acting under powers granted to it by the Council can grant block exemptions.

Article 86

Article 86 states abuse of a dominant position within the common market or a substantial part of it is prohibited if it affects trade between Member States.

In answering questions in this area it is necessary to follow the following order:

- first define the relevant market;
- secondly, having defined the market it is next necessary to consider whether the undertaking is dominant within it;
- finally, having established dominance, consider whether this dominant position has been abused.

Dominance

Before it is possible to determine whether an undertaking is dominant it is necessary to analyse the relevant market, this can be done from three perspectives:

- relevant product market;
- relevant geographical market;
- relevant temporal market.

Relevant product market

This revolves around substitutability of the product. This can be analysed from two perspectives:

- 'cross elasticity of demand' - the extent to which consumers can switch to a different product;
- 'cross elasticity of supply' - the extent to which a rival can adapt existing products or provide suitable substitutes for consumers.

Cross elasticity of demand

The relevant product market for bananas was held to be soft fruit in *United Brands* (1978) as the very old, infirm and very young are unable to switch from soft fruit to hard fruits.

Spare parts may form a separate relevant product market, if a particular brand of spare parts has to be used (*Hulin* (1979)).

The relevant market may be narrowed by the existence of sub-markets (*ITP v Commission* (1991)).

The manufacturer may have identified a separate market (*Boosey and Hawkes* (1988)).

Cross elasticity of supply

In addition to considering the extent to which it is possible for consumers to switch to different products it is also necessary to consider the extent to which the competitors can adapt products to compete (*Continental Can* (1973)).

Relevant geographical market

The relevant geographical market must be defined. This is affected by such things as ability to transport the product, homogeneity of the product, consumer tastes, conditions of competition (*Michelin* (1983)) and marketing conditions (*United Brands*).

Relevant temporal market
Competitive conditions may be affected at certain periods compared to others eg 1973-74 oil crises (*ABG Oil* (1977)).

Market power
Having defined the relevant market it is next necessary to determine whether the undertaking is dominant within it. This is done by reference to a number of criteria.

Market share
The greater the market share the greater the likelihood of dominance. The amount of market share that constitutes dominance varies enormously:

- *Commercial Solvents* 100%;
- *Continental Can* 70-80%;
- *United Brands* 45%;

the Commission have indicated that 20-40% can constitute dominance.

Barriers to entry
The greater the number of barriers to entry the harder it is for competitors to enter the market. The following have been held to be barriers to entry:

- financial resources (*Continental Can*);
- vertical integration and distribution systems (*United Brands*);
- brand loyalty;
- conduct and performance (*United Brands*);
- length of time;
- technological resources.

Abuse

A dominant position is not in itself illegal, there must be abuse of that dominant position. The following have been held to anti-competitive abuses:

- mergers (*Continental Can, Warner-Lambert/Gillette* (1993);
- predatory pricing (*AKZO* (1985));
- refusal to supply (*Commercial Solvents, Sealink/B and I-Holyhead* (1992));

- rebates (*Hoffman-La Roche* (1979), *Michelin*);
- tying (*Hilti* (1992);
- excessive prices (*United Brands*);
- exclusivity (*Tetra Pak* (1990)).

Enforcement of Articles 85 and 86

The Commission have been given wide powers of investigation under Regulation 17/62.

6 Free movement of workers

Introduction

Articles 48-51 of the EC Treaty provides for free movement of workers. Secondary legislation provides for detailed rules governing the right of entry on the territory of a Member State to carry out an economic activity; the right to remain in a Member State after having been employed there and the right to equality of access to, and conditions of, employment on the same basis as nationals of the host State. These rights are subject to exceptions contained in the Treaty concerning public policy, public safety and public health and an exemption in the case of public service.

Initially, these rights were given to 'economically active' persons and their families. The purpose being to allow economically active persons the freedom to move around the Community so that 'workers' could move to the jobs and higher wages, in other parts of the Community. Free movement of workers helped serve an economic objective and could not be regarded as an objective, in itself.

Gradually, it has been recognised that the free movement of workers includes a social dimension. The preamble to Regulation 1612/68 states that free movement is a 'fundamental right' of workers.

In 1990 freedom of movement was extended to three categories of persons who were not economically active – students, retired persons and persons of independent means. The Single European Act exhibited a greater awareness of the 'social dimension' to freedom of movement and it has now become regarded as an objective in its own right.

The Treaty on European Union establishes a European citizenship, so that every person holding the nationality of a Member State is to be a citizen of the Union under Article 8(1). *Every* citizen of the Union will have the right to move and reside freely within the territory of the Member States subject to the limitations and conditions laid down by the Treaty and by measures adopted to give it effect.

Definition of 'worker'

The term 'worker' is not defined in the Treaty. It is a Community concept and is not derived from national law. Community legislation and caselaw make it clear that a 'worker' is an employed person, irrespective of whether he or she performs managerial or manual functions.

The ECJ has given a wide definition to the term 'worker'. In *Levin v Staatssecretaris van Justitie* (1982) a chambermaid whose part time earnings fell below the Dutch minimum wage and who supplemented these earnings with her own private income and had only taken the job to obtain the right to reside in the Netherlands did come within the Community definition of 'worker'.

The applicant in *Levin* had not been a charge on the State and had supplemented her low level of earnings by her own private means. However, a person is still classified as a 'worker' if their earnings need to be augmented by supplementary benefit (*Kempf v Staatssecretaris van Justitie* (1987)). A German resident in the Netherlands who had to have his part time earnings boosted by supplementary benefit was still a 'worker'.

The definition of worker has been extended to trainees (*Lawrie-Blum v Land Baden-Württemberg* (1987)). Where the applicant was a salaried trainee teacher who initially performed her duties under supervision, but later independently, came within the definition of 'worker', the ECJ said that the test for a 'worker' was whether someone was in genuine and effective employment and performing services for an employer under his direction and control in return for remuneration.

The meaning of 'genuine and effective employment' was further considered in *Steymann* (1988). A German national joined a Bhagwan community in the Netherlands. He was a qualified plumber and performed plumbing tasks for the community and also carried out general domestic tasks and assisted in their commercial activities. He was not given formal wages but was given board, lodging and pocket money. The ECJ considered whether the work was genuine and effective and it was held that he was a worker even though he did not receive any direct remuneration. The benefits which the Community gave to its members were considered to be an indirect advantage for the work that was performed.

The employment must be a 'real' job (*Bettray* (1989)). Dutch legislation created 'social employment'. Jobs were specially created for people to support them, rehabilitate them or increase their capacity for normal work. This was done through State financed work associations, specially created for the purpose. Bettray was a German national living in Holland and was given 'social employment' as part of his treatment for drug addiction. He was receiving remuneration but was not a 'worker' as the activities could not be regarded as genuine and effective. The job had been created to fit the applicant's capacity for work, as opposed to him being selected to do a particular job.

Dependants

Members of an immigrant worker's family have the right to reside in another Member State, even if they are not workers. The spouse and children of the worker can take up employment even if they are not EU nationals.

'Family' is defined as:

- the spouse of the worker;
- children, grandchildren and other descendants, provided they are either under 21 or dependent on the worker;
- parents, grandparents and other ascendants, provided they are dependent on the worker (Article 1, Directive 68/360).

There are two types of rights. Independent immigration rights - available to workers, the self-employed, provider or recipient of services, student, retired persons or persons of independent means. Secondly, dependent immigration rights which are granted to the family of a person with an independent right.

Dependent rights cannot exist, without independent rights. Someone with an independent right to reside cannot lose that right as a result of someone else's actions but a person with a dependent right can lose their right to reside if the persons who have the independent right on whom their rights are based, gives up their rights or if the relationship ends.

Article 10(3) Regulation 1612/68 contains a provision that workers' family rights are dependent on the worker having adequate housing available. In *Commission v Germany* (1989) it was held that the housing only has to be adequate when the first family member arrives and the worker cannot be deported if it subsequently becomes inadequate.

A dependant family with parasitic rights obtain an independent right to remain if they were residing with a worker who dies and at the time of his death had acquired the right to remain in the host State or had resided continuously there for a period of two years.

The two year residence requirement does not apply if the worker died from an accident at work or an occupational illness, nor does it apply if the surviving spouse was a national of the country concerned but lost this nationality on marriage (Article 3 Regulation 1251/70 and Directive 75/34).

Co-habitees

A co-habitee's right to reside will depend on the laws of the host State (*Netherlands v Reed* (1986)). Reed was a British citizen living with her British boyfriend in the Netherlands who had obtained a right to reside there. Reed argued that, as her relationship equated with marriage, she had obtained a dependent right. The ECJ ruled that relationships outside marriage could not normally give dependent rights of residence. However, Reed was entitled to remain in Holland as, under Dutch immigration law, a non-Dutch boyfriend or girlfriend of a Dutch citizen had a right to reside. The Treaty contains a general principle of non-discrimination against Community nationals of other Member States, so on this basis Reed was entitled to reside. The case does not create a general right of residence for co-habitees. Their rights will depend on the rules of the host State.

Separated and divorced spouses

A separated spouse retains a right to reside (*Diatta* (1985)). Although separated spouses still enjoy the status of a spouse the situation could change if the parties actually divorce as in *R v Secretary of State ex p Sandhu* (1982). The House of Lords held that an Indian man who divorced his German wife lost his right to reside. The case has been criticised for the House of Lords' failure to make a preliminary reference. The ECJ refrained from considering the effect of divorce in *R v Immigration Appeal Tribunal, and Singh ex p Secretary of State for the Home Office* (1992) even though a decree nisi had been obtained at the time the UK was attempting to deport the applicant, who was the spouse of an EC national. This has been taken as grounds for believing that the ECJ intends to be generous towards divorced spouses.

Dependant can be the main breadwinner

In *Gül* a Cypriot doctor was married to a UK national and lived in Germany. He claimed that he was his wife's dependant even though his wages were substantially in excess of hers. Nevertheless, he was held to be a dependant.

Children of workers

Article 12 entitles children of workers not only the right to education but also those rights which facilitate education eg rights to grants (*Casagrande* (1974)).

Material scope

Article 48(3) provides workers with the right to enter and remain in another Member State for the purpose of employment and also to remain in that Member State after the employment has finished. These rights are in outline and have been supplemented by secondary legislation.

The right to enter

This right has been granted by Regulation 1612/68 and has been widely interpreted by the ECJ to include the right to enter in search of work as in *Procureur du Roi v Royer* (1976).

Immigrant workers who enter another Member State in search of work can remain there for a reasonable time to appraise themselves of employment opportunities. If a reasonable amount of time has elapsed and the immigrant has failed to find work then the right to residence passed. In *R v Immigration Appeal Tribunal ex p Antonissen* (1991) the ECJ considered a rule under UK immigration law which allowed immigrants six months to find work to be a reasonable length of time but the rule operated too inflexibly and those with a genuine chance of employment at the end of the period, should not be deported.

Right to reside

A worker has a right to enter a Member State to find employment but the right to a residence permit is conditional on finding employment. The right to residence is a fundamental right, which is derived from the Treaty itself and not from secondary legislation.

To gain entry to a Member State only a passport or identity card is needed (Article 3 Directive 68/360).

Article 4(2) of Directive 68/360 provides workers shall be entitled to a residence permit. Rights of residence are not conditional on the permit it is simply proof of a right of residence (*Royer* (1976)).

A worker has an absolute right of entry under Community law so it is illegal to grant only limited leave to enter (*R v Pieck* (1980)).

A full residence permit is valid for at least five years and is automatically renewable. This means that persons entitled to it reside indefinitely, unless an event occurs which terminates the right.

It is not possible to deport someone on the grounds that they failed to comply with administrative requirements on immigration as in *Watson and Belmann* (1976) and failures to obtain a residence permit may be punished only if the penalties are 'comparable to those attaching to minor offences by nationals' and can never lead to imprisonment.

Temporary and seasonal workers

A temporary worker who works from three to twelve months in another Member State is entitled to a temporary residence permit in that State to coincide with the expected period of employment (Article 6(3) Directive 68/360).

Those who work for less than three months or seasonal workers are entitled to reside in the State during the period of employment but are not entitled to a residence permit (Article 8 Directive 68/360).

The rights can be excluded to a long term or temporary worker and to a member of his family, on the ground of public policy, public security and public health.

Loss of right to reside

A temporary right to reside is lost when the purpose for which it was granted has been attained.

A full right to reside is of indefinite duration but can be lost in the following circumstances.

Departure

Absence for more than six months, other than for military service, can terminate a residence permit.

Unemployment

Article 7(1) Directive 360/68 states a residence permit may not be withdrawn from a worker solely on the ground that he is no longer in employment either because he is temporarily incapable of work as a result of illness or accident or because he is involuntarily unemployed.

This implies that the right will be lost where the worker is voluntarily unemployed. The meaning of 'voluntary' unemployment is not clear. An obvious example is where someone gives up work of their own volition and makes no attempt to find new work.

A more difficult case would be where someone gives up work voluntarily but makes reasonable efforts to find a new job perhaps for an increase in pay or for a different type of work. Can a dismissed person who was sacked due to personal misconduct be regarded as voluntarily unemployed?

Article 7(2) Directive 68/360 provides that when a residence permit is renewed for the first time, the period of residence may be restricted to not less than 12 months if the worker has been involuntarily unemployed for more than 12 consecutive months. So in this limited example involuntary unemployment may lead to a loss of a right to reside.

In *Giangregorio v Sec of State for the Home Department* (1983) it was held that the onus is on the worker to prove that he has been made involuntarily unemployed.

Access to employment/equality of treatment

There is a prohibition against discrimination on the ground of nationality which is laid down in general terms by Article 6 of the EC Treaty.

This has been held to be part of a wider principle of equality, which is a general principle of Community law (*Frilli v Belgium* (1972)); while equal treatment for migrant workers is expressly required by Article 48(2) of the EC Treaty.

These general rights have been fleshed out by secondary legislation. Articles 7-9 of Regulation 1612/68 and also the preamble to the Regulation require the abolition of:

... any discrimination based on nationality between workers of Member States as regards employment, remuneration and other conditions of work and employment.

Eligibility for employment (Articles 1-6)

Any national of a Member State has the right to take up activity as an employed person, and pursue such activity, in the territory of another Member State under the same conditions as nationals of that State (Article 1 Regulation 1612/68).

It is not possible to restrict the number or allocate a certain percentage of foreign workers to be employed in an activity or area of activity (Article 4 1612/68).

States are entitled to permit the imposition of non-nationals' conditions 'relating to linguistic knowledge required by reason of the nature of the post to be filled' (Article 3(1) Regulation 1612/68). In practice, this is one of the most important barriers to free movement; workers are inhibited from moving to other States because they do not speak the language. Article 3(1) permits a requirement of linguistic knowledge where it is required for the post.

Language requirements can be imposed where there is an official policy to promote the language as in *Groener v Minister for Education* (1989). Teachers in Irish schools are required to be proficient in the Irish language. Under the Irish constitution Irish is the first official language of Ireland and national law had a clear policy of maintaining and promoting the Irish language. The applicant was a Dutch woman who was barred from appointment as an art teacher at a college of marketing and design because she was unable to obtain the certificate; the Irish government claimed their action was justified on the basis of Article 3(1).

It was held that the EC Treaty does not prohibit the promotion by a Member State of its national language provided the measures taken to implement it are not disproportionate to the objective pursued and do not discriminate against the nationals of Member States. As teachers have a role in the promotion of the Irish language, a requirement that they have a knowledge of Irish was reasonable provided it was applied in a non-discriminatory manner and the level of knowledge to be attained must not be excessive in relation to the objective pursued.

Equality of treatment (Articles 7-9)

Article 7(1) provides that workers must be treated equally in respect of any conditions of employment and work, in particular remuneration, dismissal and should he or she become unemployed, reinstatement or re-employment.

This covers both direct and indirect discrimination. In *Ugliola* (1969) a German employer took into account, for the purposes of seniority, employees' periods of national service in Germany. The applicant had done his national service in Italy and so it did not count; and this was held to be discriminatory.

Social and tax advantages

Under Article 7(2) a migrant worker is entitled to the same 'social and tax advantages' as national workers.

The term 'social advantage' has been interpreted widely. In *Fiorini v SNCF* (1975) it was held to include a special rail reduction card to parents of large families, even though that is a benefit which does not attach to contracts of employment.

A formula was developed for determining 'social or tax advantages' in *Ministère Public v Even* (1979) which were 'those which, whether or not linked to a contract of employment, are generally granted to national workers primarily because of their objective status as workers or by virtue of the mere fact of their residence on national territory'. Applying this test Belgium did not have to pay an early retirement pension payable to ex-Belgian soldiers who were in receipt of invalidity benefit to Belgian soldiers.

Social and tax advantages do, however, include benefits granted on a discretionary basis (*Reina* (1982)). An Italian couple were living in Germany, the husband was a 'worker' and they applied for a child-birth loan which was State financed from the defendant bank. The loan was payable under German law to German nationals living in Germany. The bank argued that it was not a 'social advantage' under Article 7(2) as the loan had a political purpose as it was designed to increase the number of Germans; it was also a discretionary loan. It was argued that the loan would be hard to recover from foreign nationals who returned home. The ECJ applying the *Even* formula held that it was a social advantage and covers benefits granted on a discretionary basis.

Similarly, in *Castelli v ONPTS* (1984) an Italian, on being widowed, went to live with her son in Belgium. Applying the *Even* formula it was held that she was entitled to claim a guaranteed income paid to all old people in Belgium. She had a right to reside with her son and so was entitled to the same social and tax advantages as Belgian workers and ex-workers.

Rights of equality in the field of social and tax advantages does not apply to nationals of Member States who migrate in search of employment (*Centre Public de L'Aide Sociale de Courcelles v Lebon* (1987)). Lebon was a French national and was living and looking for work in Belgium and claimed benefit. It was held that the right to equality of treatment in the field of social and tax advantages was only for the benefit of workers and not for those who migrate in search of employment.

Vocational training

Article 7(3) entitles workers to access, under the same conditions as national workers, to training in vocational schools and re-training centres.

The extent to which this provision applied to education was considered by the ECJ in *Brown* (1988) and *Lair* (1989). Brown had obtained a place at Cambridge University, to study engineering and Lair had obtained a place at the University of Hanover to read languages and claimed grants from the UK and German authorities respectively. Although Brown had dual French/British nationality he and his family had been domiciled in France for many years. He obtained sponsorship from Ferranti and worked for them in Scotland for eight months, which was intended as a preparation for his university studies. Lair had worked intermittently in Germany for five years with spells of involuntary unemployment.

The refusal was challenged under, *inter alia*, Article 7(2) and Article 7(3) Regulation 1612/68. Advocate General Slynn said that both courses constituted vocational training under Article 7(2). The question was were Brown and Lair 'workers'? He said that a distinction should be drawn between persons who migrate genuinely in capacity as workers and those who move to another State for other purposes eg to gain work experience before studies begin. Only the former could invoke Articles 7(2) and 7(3). Although there was no minimum residence period, length of stay should be taken into account in assessing genuineness.

The court took a different view, neither course constituted 'training in vocational schools' for the purpose of Article 7(3). The parties could only succeed under Article 7(2). Brown had only acquired the status of a worker because of his acceptance into university. In Lair's case the court drew a distinction between involuntary and voluntary employment. In the latter case, the applicant could only claim a grant for a course of work if there was a link between the studies and the previous work activity.

Trade union activities

Article 8 of Regulation 1612/68 deals with discrimination in the area of trade union activities.

Workers from other Member States have a right to equal treatment as regards trade union membership and the rights that go with it eg the right to vote. They must be eligible for appointment to workers' representative bodies in the undertaking.

Immigrant workers may, under Article 8, be excluded from taking part in the management of bodies governed by public law and holding an office governed by public law.

Housing
Article 9 Regulation 1612/88 gives immigrant Community workers the right to equal treatment with regard to housing, including public housing. This would bar any rule precluding them from putting their name down for eg council housing.

Right to remain
Regulation 1251/70 permits a worker to remain permanently in a Member State in which he has worked on retirement, incapacity or if he is a 'frontier' worker.

Retirement
A worker requires a right of residence on retirement provided:
- he has reached the age laid down by the law of that Member State for entitlement to an old age pension;
- he has been employed in the host State for at least 12 months;
- he has resided continuously in the host State for more than three years.

Incapacity
If a worker has resided continuously in a State for more than two years and stops working as a result of a permanent incapacity, then that worker has a permanent right to reside.

If the permanent incapacity is a result of an accident at work, or an occupational disease entitling him to a pension for which an institution of the host State is responsible, there are no conditions as to length of service.

Frontier workers
A worker who, after three years' continuous employment in the territory of that State, works as an employed person in another Member State, while retaining his residence in the territory of the first State, to which he returns, as a rule, each day or at least once a week, has a right to reside.

A worker's family have a right to remain in the host State after the worker's death (see p 170).

Exceptions

Article 48(3) allows an exception from the free movement of workers provisions where it is justified on the ground of public policy, public security or public health.

Article 48(3) is further fleshed out by Directive 64/221. Article 3 provides that measures taken on the ground of public policy or public security shall be based on the personal conduct of the individual concerned.

Meaning of 'public policy'

In *Van Duyn v Home Office* (1974) it was said that the concept of public policy is subject to control by Community institutions but the definition of public policy can vary from State to State.

In *Rutili v French Minister of the Interior* (1975) it was held that for the public policy exception to be invoked the threat must be genuine and serious. Restrictions are subject to the proportionality principle.

In *R v Bouchereau* (1977) the test was expressed as a genuine and sufficiently serious threat to the requirements of public policy affecting one of the fundamental principles of society. Directive 64/221 lays down that public policy shall not be involved:

* 'to serve economic ends' (Article 2(2));
* previous criminal conviction shall not in themselves constitute grounds for taking measures (Article 3(2));
* expiry of the identity card or passport used by the person concerned to enter the host country and to obtain a residence permit shall not justify exclusion from the territory (Article 3(3)).

Meaning of 'personal conduct'

In *Van Duyn v Home Office* (1974) it was held that present association with a group or organisation could count towards personal conduct but that past association never could.

Van Duyn was a Dutch national, who was refused entry into the UK on the ground of public policy. She wished to take up employment with the Church of Scientology. Scientology was not illegal but was considered socially undesirable by the UK government. The refusal was based on personal conduct due to the applicant's association with the Scientology sect. The case was the first preliminary reference made by a court of the UK and the controversial result has been explained as an attempt by the ECJ to be accommodate the UK on its first reference.

The ECJ held that conduct does not have to be illegal to justify exclusion but must be socially harmful and administrative measures must have been taken to counteract activities.

The ECJ has, after *Van Duyn*, laid down much stricter tests. In *R v Boucherau* (1977) a French national resident in the UK who had twice been convicted of drugs offences was deported from the UK. It was held that previous convictions should only be taken into account if there was a present threat to requirements of public policy but past conduct alone could constitute a threat if it was sufficiently grave.

In *Adoui v Cornuaille* (1982) two French waitresses were working in a bar in Belgium but were also working as prostitutes. Prostitution was legal in Belgium but discouraged. The Belgian authorities denied them a residence permit.

It was held that Member States could not deny residence to non-nationals because of conduct which, when attributable to a State's own nationals, did not give rise to repressive measures or other genuine and effective measures to combat such conduct.

In *Bonsignore* (1975) an Italian living in Germany was deported after conviction of a criminal offence as a deterrent. It was held that a deportation order can only be made in connection with breaches of peace and public security which may be committed by the individual concerned.

Procedural rights

Article 9 Directive 64/221 provides that a person shall not be deported until an opinion has been received from a competent authority of the host country before taking the decision. The competent authority must be separate from the authority taking the decision.

In *Santillo* (1980) a trial judge's recommendation to deport after a prison term was completed did amount to an 'opinion' under Article 9 but the opinion was not sufficiently proximate in time to the decision recommending deportation.

Public service exemption

Free movement of workers does not apply to public service under Article 48(4). This could be a very significant exemption but has been interpreted narrowly.

In *Commission v Belgium* (public employees) (1979) all posts in the 'public service' were limited to Belgian nationals, nurses etc. The

Belgian government argued that those jobs were within the public service. The ECJ disagreed and held that it only applied to the exercise of official authority and it only applied to employees who were safeguarding the general interests of the State. Lower levels should be assimilated even though they could be barred promotion to higher posts. Such a bar would be legal.

Revision Notes

Definition of 'worker'

The term is not defined in the Treaty. It is a Community concept and is not derived from national law. The ECJ have given a wide definition:

- a part time worker who supplemented her wages from her private income was a 'worker' (*Levin* (1982));
- a part time worker whose earnings were supplemented by supplementary benefit was a 'worker' (*Kempf* (1987));
- a trainee has come within the definition of 'worker' (*Lawrie-Blum* (1987)) the test was stated as being genuine and effective employment and performing services for an employer under his direction and control in return for remuneration;
- a worker who received payment in kind was a 'worker' (*Steymann* (1988));
- a job created especially for a person and is tailor made to suit his own characteristics does not make that person a 'worker' (*Bettray* (1988).

Dependants

'Family' is defined as:

- the spouse of the worker;
- children, grandchildren and other descendants (if either under 21 or dependent on the worker);
- parents, grandparents and other ascendants (provided they are dependent on the worker). (Article 1 Directive 68/360).

A dependant who has a parasitic right on a worker obtains an independent right right if:

- they were residing with the worker at the date of the death;
- the worker had, at date of death, acquired the right to reside in the host State or had resided continuously there for two years.

The rights of co-habitees depend on the law of the Member State but it is not possible to discriminate against the co-habitees of a foreign worker compared to nationals of the Member State (*Reed* (1986)).

A separated spouse still has a right to reside (*Diatta* (1985)). It appears that a divorced spouse does not have a right to reside (*R v Secretary of State ex p Sandhu* (1982). A dependant can be the main breadwinner (*Gül*).

Material scope

Article 48(3) provides the right to enter and remain in another Member State for the purpose of employment and remain in the other Member State once employment has terminated.

Right to enter

Regulation 1612/68 fleshes out the rights laid down in Article 48(3).

It includes the right to enter to search for work (*Royer* (1976)). Entrants have a reasonable amount of time to find work (*R v Immigration Appeal Tribunal ex p Antonissen* (1991)).

Right to reside

There is an absolute right of residence under Community law (*Pieck* (1980)).

A residence permit is evidence of a right to reside and the right is not conditional upon it (*Royer* (1976)).

It is not possible to deport someone on the ground of failure to comply with administrative requirements (*Watson and Belmann* (1976).

Loss of right to reside

Loss of right to reside can take place in the following circumstances:

* departure – absence for more than six months (other than military service);
* unemployment – the right will be lost where a worker is voluntarily unemployed;
* involuntary unemployment – where the worker has been out of a work for a consecutive 12 months.

Access to employment/equality of treatment

There are general principles of non-discrimination in Community law. Article 6 (formerly Article 7) of the EC Treaty prohibits discrimination on the ground of nationality. There is also a general principle of equality (*Frilli* (1972)).

These general rights have been fleshed out by Articles 7-9 of Regulation 1612/68.

Language requirements can be imposed where there is an official policy to promote the language (*Groener* (1989)).

Social and tax advantages

Every migrant worker has the right to the same 'social and tax advantages' as national workers.

'Social advantages' include all benefits received as a result of having performed the job in question (*Fiorini* (1979)).

The test for determining 'social and tax advantages' has been laid down in *Even* (1979) as:

... those which, whether or not linked to a contract of employment, are generally granted to national workers ... because of their objective status as workers or by virtue of ... their residence on national territory.

Social and tax advantages includes discretionary benefits (*Reina* (1982)).

Right to equality in respect of social and tax advantages do not extend to those who are searching for work (*Lebon* (1987)).

Vocational training

Article 7(3) of Regulation 1612/68 entitles workers to access to training in vocational schools and retraining centres on the same basis as national workers.

These rights do not extend to students or the voluntary unemployed (*Brown* (1988) and *Lair* (1989)).

Trade union activities

Workers from another Member State have the right to equal treatment with respect to trade union activities (Article 8 Regulation 1612/68).

Housing

Migrant workers have the right to equal treatment in housing (Article 9 Regulation 1612/68).

Right to remain

A worker has a right to remain in the host State on retirement, incapacity and if he is a frontier worker. The right also applies to the family of a worker who has died if the worker had a right to remain on death or had resided continuously for two years. This does not apply if a worker died from an accident at work or an occupational illness, or if surviving spouse lost nationality of host State on marriage (Regulation 1251/70).

Exceptions

Article 48(3) allows exceptions on the ground of public policy, public security and public health. This has been fleshed out by Directive 64/221.

Public policy has been defined as a genuine and serious threat (*Rutili* (1975)) and a genuine and sufficiently serious threat to the requirements of public policy affecting one of the fundamental principles of society (*R v Bouchereau* (1977)).

Previous convictions should only be taken into account if they constitute a present threat to the requirements of public policy (*Boucherau* (1977)).

Residence permits can only be denied to migrant workers if repressive measures are taken against the host State's nationals for the same type of activity (*Adoui* (1981)).

Public service exemption

This only applies to the exercise of official authority and to employees who are safeguarding the interests of the State (*Commission v Belgium* (public employees) (1979)).

7 EC sex equality legislation

You should be familiar with the following areas: ✓

ESSENTIALS

- Article 119 equal pay for equal work
- Directive 75/117 on equal pay for work of equal value
- Directive 76/207 Equal Treatment Directive for Men and Women in Employment
- Directive 79/7 Equal Treatment Directive in matters of social security
- Directive 86//378 equal treatment for occupational pension schemes
- UK opt out from agreement annexed to social protocol

At the outset it is important to distinguish between direct discrimination and indirect discrimination. Direct discrimination is where similar situations are treated differently or different situations are treated alike; this is always illegal unless permitted by one of the derogations from the equal treatment principle. Indirect discrimination refers to neutral criteria which has a greater adverse effect on one sex compared to another. This is not an absolute principle and will be legal where it can be objectively justified and satisfies the principle of proportionality.

Article 119

Direct effect of Article 119

In *Defrenne v Belgium (No 1)* (1971), the Advocate General indicated that Article 119 was capable of giving rise to rights to individuals.

This was confirmed by the Court in *Defrenne v Sabena (No 2)*. However, the ECJ seemed to make a distinction between direct and indirect discrimination:

within the whole area of application of Article 119 between, first, direct and overt discrimination which may be identified solely with the aid of the criteria based on equal work and equal pay referred to in [Article 119] and, secondly indirect and disguised discrimination which can be identified by reference to more explicit implementing [legislation].

It was also held that Article 119 had horizontal and vertical direct effect. The apparent argument that Article 119 only has direct effect insofar as the claim relates to direct discrimination has been interpreted as meaning that Article 119 cannot be relied on where the claim involves the assessment of criteria which cannot be taken into account by a court.

In the interests of legal certainty the effect of the judgment was limited, so that claims for backdated pay could only be made from the date of judgment, unless a claim had already been brought.

What is 'pay' for the purposes of Article 119?

In *Defrenne v Belgium (No 1)* (1971) it was held that social security compulsory pension schemes which lack any element of agreement and apply to general categories of workers fall outside the meaning of 'pay' for the purposes of Article 119. Criticism of *Defrenne (No 1)* test has been:

- that it discriminates between employees whose employers operate one form of pension scheme rather than another;
- the operation of Article 119 may be dependent on the national organisation of pension schemes.

Contributions to a private occupational scheme which has 'contracted out' of a State scheme constitutes 'pay' within the meaning of Article 119 (*Worringham and Humphreys v Lloyds Bank Limited* (1981)).

The first of a number of exceptions to *Defrenne (No 1)* was laid down in *Liefting v Academisch Ziekenhuis bij Universiteit van Amsterdam* (1984). Contributions to a State social security scheme affected the level of gross pay and therefore the level of other benefits did constitute 'pay' for the purpose of Article 119.

Barber v Guardian Royal Exchange Assurance Group (1990) held that Article 119 applied to employers' contracted out occupational pension schemes and to all redundancy payments. The inclusion of statutory redundancy payments was the latest exception to the *Defrenne (No 1)* principle and was confirmed with regard to 'top up' redundancy payments for workers between 60 and 65 in *Commission v Belgium* (1993). Discrimination in pensionable ages in relation to occupational pension schemes was also held to be 'pay' within Article 119 and therefore illegal.

The ruling in *Barber* was said not to be retroactive. However, there was ambiguity as to the meaning of this limitation of the temporal effect of the *Barber* judgment. An employee could not bring a claim 'with effect from a date prior to that of this judgment', unless proceedings had been entered into prior to that date. Did this mean that the equal treatment principle applied only to benefits for periods after the date of judgment or to benefits for periods before judgment but payable afterwards? It was held in *Ten Oever v Stichting Bedrijfspensionenenfonds voor het Glazenwassers-en Schoonmaakbedrjf* (1993) that Article 119 could only be invoked for periods of employment after the date of the *Barber* judgement. A protocol to the Treaty on European Union provides that the *Barber* judgment will only apply to periods of employment after the date of judgment.

Ten Oever was confirmed in *Neath v Hugh Steeper Ltd* (1993) which added that Article 119 could not be invoked to challenge the financial basis of pension rights which accrued before 17 May 1990.

Further clarification of the *Barber* judgment was obtained in *Coloroll Pension Trustees Ltd v Russell* (1994). It was held that Article 119 applied to pensions paid under a trust, even though pension fund trustees are not parties to the employment relationship. Trustees are still under this obligation to observe Article 119, even if this is contrary to the trust deed. The equal treatment principle also applies to employers who have transferred their acquired rights from another pension fund which has not observed Article 119. This means that pension fund trustees may have to make good the cost of another company failing to comply with Article 119.

Article 119 does not apply to working conditions

In *Defrenne v Sabena (No 3)* (1978) it was held that Article 119 does not stretch to equality of working conditions other than pay between men and women. Consequently, an attempt to use Article 119 as a means of ensuring equality of retirement ages failed.

Similarly in *Burton v British Railways Board* (1982), access to a voluntary early retirement redundancy scheme, where women could apply earlier than men, is governed by the equal treatment directive and not by Article 119.

'Pay' includes non-contractual benefits

Benefits need only be granted in respect of employment, to come within Article 119, even if there is no contractual obligation to provide them (*Garland v British Rail Engineering Limited* (1982)). Special travel facilities provided to retired male workers and their families which are not available to retired female employees and their families are 'pay' within Article 119. Similarly, Article 119 applies to lump sum payments made to dependants of an employee who has died in service (*Coloroll*).

Collective bargaining

In *Enderby v Frenchay Health Authority* (1993) it was held that where an occupation which was carried out predominately by women, but where men performing different jobs but of equal value were paid more and the difference had been caused by separate collective bargaining processes, the onus is on the employer to show that the difference is objectively justified. The fact that the difference has been caused by separate collective bargaining processes cannot be sufficient objective justification. It was for national courts to decide whether difficulties in recruitment constituted objective justification.

Part time workers

The cases relating to part time workers have developed the law relating to indirect discrimination. Provisions which treat part time workers adversely are not *prima facie* discriminatory as they affect both sexes. However, as part time workers are predominantly women such provisions will have a greater adverse impact on them.

In *Jenkins v Kingsgate (Clothing Productions) Ltd* (1981) it was held that a variation in pay between full time and part time workers does not breach Article 119 provided the hourly rates are applied without distinction based on sex and differences are 'objectively justified', this imported the concept of the employer's intention. It is rarely the employer's intention to discriminate but rather to gain a commercial advantage through the use of cheap labour. *Jenkins* was interpreted by the English courts as meaning that if the employer's intention had been commercial advantage then that was objectively justified discrimination. This would have made it difficult for part time workers to succeed under Article 119.

The effects of *Jenkins* were mitigated by *Bilka-Kaufhaus*, the ECJ held that it is for a national court to determine whether a policy is objectively justified but it was limited by the principle of proportionality and the employer has to show:

- that the policy meets a genuine need of the enterprise;
- was suitable for attaining the objective set;
- was necessary for the purpose.

Statutory sick pay was held to come within Article 119 in *Rinner-Kühn v FWW Spezial - Gebaudereinigung GmbH and Co* (1989). National legislation which allowed for differences between full and part workers was illegal. The principle that legislation can be a source of indirect discrimination has enormous consequences for the UK as can be seen by the case of *R v Secretary of State for Employment ex p Equal Opportunities Commission* (1994) where the House of Lords held that provisions of the Employment Protection (Consolidation) Act 1978 which prevented part time workers from claiming redundancy payments and compensation for unfair dismissal were not objectively justified and consequently illegal.

Rinner-Kühn is also significant in that, although the question of objective justification is left to national courts, the ECJ is prepared to set down limits as to what can constitute justification. In particular, it will look at the merits of justification arguments. So in *Rinner-Kühn* the German government could not argue that part time workers are less dependent on their earnings than full time workers.

Significant guidance as to the merits of objective justification arguments, in relation to small employers, was provided by the ECJ in a case under the Equal Treatment Directive in *Kirsammer-Hack v Sidal* (1993), when it was held that exclusion from employment protection for part time employees of firms which had less than five employees was objectively justified on the ground that it lightened the administrative, financial and legal burdens on small firms.

Three recent German cases have also extended the rights of part time workers. In *Kowalska v Freie und Hansestadt Hamburg* (1990) a provision of a collective agreement excluding part time workers from severance pay infringed Article 119. The court also held that the national court must amend indirectly discriminatory provisions of collective agreements as opposed to simply declaring them void.

In *Nimz v Freie und Hansestadt Hamburg* (1991) part time workers had to work twice as long for re-classification to a higher grade than full time workers. The ECJ held that in showing experience is an objective factor that leads to improvement in performance it would have to show that for that particular job additional experience was required in order to produce better performance.

Different problems arose in *Arbeiterwohlfahrt der Stadt Berlin eV v Botel* (1992) the applicant took paid time off to attend training classes. The length of the classes exceeded her working hours but she was only compensated for her normal working hours. This lead to her being paid less than full time workers for attending the same course. The ECJ said that the difference in pay could not be objectively justified as it would discourage part time workers from undergoing training.

It has been recently held that part time workers have the right to join a pension fund unless their exclusion can be objectively justified (*Vroege v NCIV (1994)*). Furthermore, the right can be backdated to 8 April 1976, which is the date of judgment in *Defrenne (No 2)*. However, it was held in *Fisscher v Voorhuis Hengelo BV* (1994) that where a pension scheme requires contributions from employees, then contributions can be demanded from an employee who wishes to backdate membership of the scheme for that period.

What is equal work?

Article 119 is not limited to situations where the man and the woman are contemporaneously employed (*Macarthys v Smith* (1980)). The applicant was paid less for the same job as her male predecessor had been paid. The ECJ also rejected the need for the adoption of a 'hypothetical male' the parallels could be drawn on the basis of 'concrete appraisals of work actually performed by employees of different sex within the establishment or service'.

'Equal work' enables applicants to compare themselves to other groups of workers who have had their work rated as inferior but still receive more pay (*Murphy v An Bord Telecom Eireann* (1987)).

Equal pay Directive

Article 1 defines the principle of equal pay as being 'the same work or for work to which equal value is attributed'. This has been held as restating the equal pay principle in Article 119. So if a national court can identify discrimination solely by reference to Article 119 then it will be directly effective. If discrimination can only be identified by additional criteria then reliance will be placed on the Directive (or its implementing provisions).

Initially, the UK implemented legislation that provided equal pay was required where a man and woman were employed on 'like work' and 'work was rated as equivalent' on the basis of a job evaluation undertaken with the consent of an employer. This was held to be a breach of the Directive in *Commission v UK* 61/81 as there had been a failure to provide a means whereby claims of equal value might be assessed in the absence of a job evaluation scheme. As a result the Equal Pay (Amendment) Regulations 1983 were passed and an industrial tribunal now has the power to have a report prepared to determine whether something is of equal value.

Commission v Denmark case 143/83 allows for comparisons to be made with work of equal value in different establishments which are covered by the same collective agreement.

In *Rummler v Dato-Druck GmbH* (1987) a job evaluation scheme was challenged as the criteria it assessed included *inter alia* muscular effort. This was held not to be discriminatory so long as:

- the system as a whole precluded discrimination;
- the criteria used are objectively justified.

To be objectively justified they must:

- be appropriate to the tasks carried out;
- correspond to a genuine need of the undertaking.

In *Handels-OG Kontorfunktionaerernes Forbund I Danmark v Dansk Arbejdsgiverforening ex p Danfoss* (1989) criteria such as 'flexibility' and 'seniority' could be taken into account in assessing pay. However, there were conditions attached to the ability to invoke 'flexibility'. If it meant that it was an assessment of the employee's work and women received less payment than men, then, *prima facie*, there would be discrimination and the onus would be on the employer to prove that the difference was objectively justified.

Danfoss is also interesting as it appears to accept 'seniority' as a reason to give more pay. This is hard to reconcile with *Nimz* where it was held that for 'seniority' to be taken into account it would have to be shown that longer experience leads to better performance in the particular job.

Equality of treatment Directive

Scope of the Directive

Male and female workers must receive equal treatment in access to employment, vocational training and promotion in respect of working conditions.

Equality of access

Equality of access to employment
This was considered in *Dekker v Stichting Vormingscentrum Voor Jonge Volwassenen* (1991). The applicant's offer of employment was withdrawn when the employer discovered that she was pregnant. The employer argued that the intention had not been to discriminate, there had been financial reasons behind the move, as he would not have recovered the cost of the maternity benefit from the Dutch social fund. Nevertheless, it was held to be a breach of the Directive.

Ellis 31 (1994) CML Rev 43-75 argues that *Dekker* creates an extension to the idea of direct discrimination. The reason the applicant was not recruited was because she was pregnant, as only a woman can become pregnant her sex was the cause of her failure to get the job. A causation test had been introduced to the concept of direct discrimination. Also, there was no actual male comparator in this case so it may signal a change of mind on the question of hypothetical comparators after *Macarthys v Smith*.

By contrast in *Handels-OG Kontorfunktionaerernes Forbund I Danmark v Dansk Arbejdsgiverforening (ex p Aldi Marked K/S)* (1990) it was held that the applicant had not been unfairly dismissed for absences from work due to illness caused by a pregnancy two years earlier. The court said that after maternity leave, illness due to pregnancy should be treated like any other. The question then was whether she had suffered adverse treatment compared to a male employee.

Dismissal on grounds of pregnancy was again found to be discriminatory in *Webb v EMO Air Cargo (UK) Ltd* (1994). The applicant had been employed to replace another employee who had become pregnant. Two weeks after starting the post the applicant herself became pregnant and was dismissed. Following *Dekker*, the dismissal was held to be illegal by the ECJ.

Equality of access to vocational training
In *Danfoss* (1989) it was held that there was no discrimination where vocational training has been offered to a group of workers who are predominantly male, where there was an objective reason for offering it to them. In this case, it was shown that the vocational training was necessary for the tasks which had been allotted to the predominantly male employees.

Collective agreements
Article 4 provides that provisions contrary to the equal treatment principle in collective agreements, internal rules of undertakings or rules governing the independent occupations and professions are to be nullified or amended by the courts.

In *Commission v UK* case 165/82 (1983) it was held that this applies to non-legally binding agreements, as well as binding agreements.

Equality of working conditions
Article 5 provides for the application of the equal treatment principle to working conditions.

Conditions governing dismissal

Article 5 specifically states that working conditions include dismissal.

Access to a voluntary redundancy scheme comes within the meaning of dismissal for the purposes of Article 5 (*Burton v British Railways Board* (1982)). The applicant did not succeed in his claim, as under Article 7(1) of the social security Directive, it is possible to exclude from the equal treatment principle the pensionable ages for men and women. Women could apply to the voluntary redundancy scheme at the age of 50, whereas men had to wait until 55, as the ages were linked to the statutory retirement ages for men and women it was held to be legal.

Article 7 does not apply where retirement age is calculated for 'other purposes' ie purposes other than eligibility for State pension (*Marshall v Southampton and South West Hampshire AHA (Teaching) (No 1)* (1984)); (*Beets - Proper v Landschot Bankiers* (1986)). In both cases the applicants had been forced to retire at 60 whereas men could carry on until they were 65. The ages were linked to statutory retirement ages. The ECJ held that neither case concerned access to a pension scheme and was therefore prepared to draw a distinction between age limits for dismissal (which comes within Article 5) and age limits for pensions (which is caught by the exemption for pensionable ages).

Marshall (No 1) is also noteworthy as the ECJ held that Directives could not have horizontal direct effect. (See Chapter 2).

Adoption leave is not a working condition

In *Commission v Italy* case 163/82 (1983) the Commission took enforcement proceedings in respect of an Italian law that provided for eligibility for women but not men for three months compulsory leave after a child under the age of six was adopted into the family. This was held to be legal by the ECJ, as they felt it was necessary to assimilate conditions of entry of an adopted child into the family to those of a newborn child. The judgment did not follow Advocate General Rozes' opinion. She argued that the paramount aim of adoption leave is to secure the emotional ties between the child and the adoptive family. This is a task that can be performed equally as well by the father as the mother and therefore in the Advocate General's opinion it is a working condition.

Derogations from the equal treatment principle

As derogations depart from individual rights they must all be interpreted strictly (*Johnston v Chief Constable of the Royal Ulster Constabulary* (1986)). They are also subject to the principle of proportionality.

Where sex is a determining factor

Article 2(2) authorises Member States to exempt occupational activities 'for which the sex of the worker constitutes a determining factor'. This has been defined by the Commission to mean that there are 'objective reasons ... [which mean] the job can be carried out either only by a man or only by a woman.'

This article needs to be read in conjunction with Article 9(2) which requires Member States to periodically assess the occupational activities excluded in order to decide, in the light of social developments, whether there is a justification for continuing with the exclusions concerned. This list is under the supervision of the Commission as Member States are required to submit a list of restricted occupations to them. Certain jobs require physical characteristics which determine that the job can only be done by one sex or the other eg actor/actress, model, wet nurse etc.

The derogation has operated in a wider context than this, however, to include jobs which social and cultural conditioning have resulted in the job being performed by one particular sex, for example, midwives, firemen etc. The function of Article 9 is to review social developments to assess whether attitudes have changed to a sufficient extent to enable certain occupational activities to be opened up to both sexes.

The significance of permitting social considerations into account is that they vary from State to State. Consequently, there is an element of discretion in the hands of a Member State as to what activities constitute excluded activities for the purpose of Article 9 (2). This discretion is fettered as Article 9 (2) list must be submitted to the Commission who are, therefore, able to exercise supervision over it. Failure to produce a list will be a breach of the Directive as in case 248/83 *Commission v Germany* (1985).

The environment played a crucial part in the outcome of *Johnston.* The applicant had been refused a renewal of her contract as a member of the RUC full time reserve and to be allowed training in the handling and use of firearms. The reasons given for the refusal were that it was necessary for safeguarding public security and to protect public safety and public order.

The ECJ held that regard had to be paid to the context in which an armed police force carries out its activities, which is determined by the environment. Arming women police officers in Northern Ireland places them under a greater risk of assassination than if they are left unarmed. It was therefore contrary to the interests of public safety to provide women officers with arms. On this basis sex was a determining factor in the carrying out of certain police activities.

The ECJ said that even where a situation came within a derogation there was an obligation firstly, under Article 9 (2) to periodically assess whether the derogation could still be maintained. Secondly, as this was a derogation from an individual right the principle of proportionality must be observed. There would have to be a balancing between the interests of equal treatment and public safety and it was for the national court to determine whether an action was proportionate or not.

This part of the ruling has been criticised by Prechal and Burrows in *Gender Discrimination Law of the European Community*. They felt that there was nothing in the evidence which suggested that armed women police offices were more likely to be assassinated than male officers. The Chief Constable had not, for example, asserted that armed women were more likely to provoke an armed response. By allowing questions of environment to be invoked, considerations other than biological differences and social considerations would be taken into account. Female police officers have since been armed in Northern Ireland.

In *Commission v UK* 165/82 (1983) the Commission challenged the UK's exclusion under s 6 (3) of the Sex Discrimination Act from the equal treatment principle of employment in a private household or small undertakings where the number of persons does not exceed five. The Commission also challenged the UK's prohibition on men applying for employment or training as midwives. The UK government argued that the exclusions came within Article 2(2).

The ECJ objected to the general nature of the domestic service and small business exceptions. Although there are particular jobs in both sectors which can only be performed by one particular sex, this does not justify exempting them entirely from the equal treatment principle. This was echoed in *Johnston* where it was again held that a woman could only be excluded from specific activities.

The exclusion relating to midwives was found to be legal. The ECJ referred to Article 9 (2) and the need to constantly review excluded occupational activities in the light of social developments. It was held that the exclusion was appropriate given personal sensitivities, which existed at the date of judgment. These personal sensitivities were capable of making sex a determining factor for the occupational activity. The judgment was contrary to Advocate General Rozes' opinion who thought that there was nothing in being a midwife itself which justified the exclusion and laid emphasis on the patient's right to choose the midwife she prefers. The UK has since allowed men to become midwives.

Recruitment problems arose in case 318/86 *Commission v France*. Separate recruitment took place for the French prison service. The

Commission agreed that separate appointment to lower grades within the service was justified under Article 2 (2) but objected to the fact that promotion to the higher grade of governor was discriminatory, as this role could be performed by a man or a woman. Yet a governor could only be appointed from the ranks of prison wardens for which there was separate recruitment. The ECJ held that there might be reasons for needing the experience of having been a warden in the prison before being appointed a governor and therefore the separate recruitment was legal.

There have been a string of cases relating to night work. In *Stoeckel* (1991) a German ban on night work for women, which purportedly protected women, was held to be illegal. However, the situation is different where restrictions have been imposed on women performing night work in order to comply with International Treaties. French restrictions on night work by women in industry were permissible when it resulted from international obligations concluded prior to the EC Treaty (*Ministère Public v Levy*). The ECJ urged a Belgian court in *Office Nationale de l'Emploi v Minne* (1994) which faced similar Belgian restrictions to make sure that they had only been imposed to the extent that was necessary for international obligations.

Protection of women, in particular with regard to pregnancy and maternity
Article 2 para 3 provides for the second exception to the equal treatment principle whereby provisions are allowed which are for the protection of women, particularly with regard to pregnancy and maternity.

In *Hofmann v Barmer Ersatzkasse* (1984) questions relating to the interpretation of Article 2(3) arose. German legislation provided for two successive periods of maternity leave after the birth of a child. The first leave is compulsory and covers a period for eight weeks after childbirth and the second leave is optional and covers the period from the end of the first leave until the child has reached the age of six months old. A sickness fund pays the mother a daily allowance during the period of the leave.

The applicant was a father of a baby and applied to the fund for the allowance in respect of the second period, while his girlfriend returned to work. The authorities replied that the legislation specifically excluded the possibility of paternity leave. The ECJ said that the purpose behind Article 2 (3) was twofold:

* to protect the mother's biological condition during pregnancy and after pregnancy until her physiological and mental functions return to normal;

- to protect the special relationship between mother and child by preventing that relationship being disturbed by multiple burdens.

On this basis the optional period of maternity leave fell within Article 2(3) as it was seeking to protect the mother. The ECJ said that it was within the discretion of the Member State as to the nature and the detailed implementation of protective measures. This was contrary to the Commission's wish that Article 2 (3) be interpreted as strictly as possible. The ECJ's decision has been criticised by Prechal and Burrows, on the following grounds:

- there is no indication as to the length of period needed to protect the mother's relationship with the child;
- too much discretion is left to the Member States, in the implementation of the rules protecting the mother;
- the aim of protecting the mother against multiplicity of burdens can be achieved by giving the optional leave to the father; as the mother would be relieved of domestic burdens. Protection against multiplicity of burdens can therefore be achieved by non-discriminatory methods;
- the Directive is not designed to organise family relationships and yet no choice is given in the division of work between home and family. The father must work and the mother must remain at home.

In *Johnston* it was again said that the purpose of Article 2 (3) was to protect the biological condition of the mother and the mother's relationship with the child. It could not therefore be invoked where there is a general risk which is not specific to women, such as the threat to public order in Northern Ireland, where the risks would apply equally to men and women.

A stricter interpretation of Article 2(3) occurred in *Commission v France* 312/86 (1989). The French Labour Code allowed for the extension of maternity leave, reduced working hours, additional holidays at the start of the school year, allowances for a creche or babysitters, reduced retirement age and additional benefits for children of working mothers only.

This was held to contravene Article 2 (3), special rights accorded to the mother after pregnancy and childbirth fall outside Article 2 (3). It can be deduced from this case that 'maternity' only applies to the period immediately after childbirth and not to any longer period when the child may have started at school.

Positive discrimination

Article 2 (4) provides for positive action on behalf of women. It has been interpreted strictly and the ECJ will only permit positive discrimination where it can be shown that inequalities actually exist (case 312/86 *Commission v France*). Measures are also only be of a temporary duration as they are subject to review under Article 9(2).

The concept of positive discrimination in Community law has been extended by its inclusion in the agreement annexed to the social protocol of the Treaty on European Union. Article 6(3) allows for measures of positive discrimination and does not require prior establishment of illegality and is not subject to Article 9 (2) limitations.

Effective remedies

Starting with the cases of *Von Colson and Kamann v Land Nordrhein - Westfalen* (1984) and *Harz v Deutsche Tradax* (1984) it can be seen that the Directive requires real and effective sanctions where there has been a breach of the equal treatment principle. Although there is no express provision to this effect in the Directive, Article 6 requires the Member States to introduce measures so that applicants, who feel wronged by the failure to apply the equal treatment to them, can pursue their claims by judicial process. From this the ECJ has adduced the need for effective sanctions and said in its judgment in *Von Colson* that: 'it is impossible to establish real equality of opportunity without an appropriate system of sanctions'.

This has wider implications for Community law and the principle has been extended in *Francovich al Bonifaci v Italian Republic* (see Chapter 2).

More recently, the principle has been applied in relation to British legislation in *Marshall v Southampton and South West Hampshire Area Health Authority (Teaching) (No 2)* (1993). An arbitrary upper limit of £6,250 in the Sex Discrimination Act 1975 for the victim of discrimination was held to be contrary to Article 6 of the Equal Treatment Directive. The ECJ held that where financial compensation is the method of fulfilling the Directive's objectives it must enable the financial loss and damage actually suffered to be made good. In this respect the judgment differed from the Advocate General Gerven's opinion which had stated that although the damages must be 'adequate' it did not have to be equal to the damage suffered. The court also said that an award of damages could not leave out matters such as 'effluxion of time' that might reduce the value of the award, therefore interest was payable on the damages.

Procedural remedies

In addition to substantive remedies such as damages a case under the social security Directive *(Emmott v Minister of Social Welfare* (1991)) held that it is also necessary to create effective procedural remedies. In that case it was held that limitation periods do not start to run until a Directive is properly implemented.

Interpretive obligation on Member States

It was said in *Von Colson* that Member States must interpret national legislation in accordance with the aims and purposes of the Directive, 'in so far as is possible.' Again this is a principle which has a wider application than equality law and has been extended in *Marleasing v La Comercial* (see Chapter 2).

Principle of equal treatment in matters of social security

The Equal Treatment Directive provides for further legislation for the progressive implementation of the equal treatment principle in relation to social security.

The social security Directive itself provides for the progressive implementation of the equal treatment into the field of social security and contains many important exceptions.

Personal and material scope of the Directive

Personal scope

The social security Directive applies to the 'working population' which includes:

self employed persons, workers and self employed persons whose activity is interrupted by illness, accident or involuntary unemployment and persons seeking employment' and 'retired or invalided workers and self employed persons'.

It was held in *Drake v Adjudication Officer* (1985) that 'working population' included someone who had interrupted work to look after an invalid mother. It was also held that, provided the benefit was included in the risks covered, it could come within the equal treatment principle even though the benefit is paid to a third party.

By contrast, in *Johnson v Adjudication Officer* (1991) it was held that a woman who had given up work to care for her children and was unable to resume work because of illness did not come within the Directive unless she actively looks for work. While in *Achterberg-te*

Riele v Sociale Verzekeringsbank, Amsterdam (1989) a woman who has never engaged in paid work or given up paid work to care for a family does not come within the Directive.

Material scope
The Directive applies to:

* statutory schemes providing protection against the following risks: sickness, invalidity, old age, accidents at work or occupational diseases and unemployment;
* social assistance intended to supplement or replace the schemes referred to above.

Family and survivors' benefits are not covered. In *R v Secretary of State ex p Smithson* (1992) it was held that the 'benefit had to be directly and effectively linked to the protection provided against any of the risks specified in Article 3 (1)'.

Consequently, housing benefit, which was linked to a notional, as opposed to an actual income, does not come within the terms of the Directive.

Similarly, it was held in *Jackson v Chief Adjudication Officer* (1993) income support or supplementary benefit does not come within the terms of the Directive as it is a general, subsistence benefit and does not cover the risks outlined in Article 3(1). Consequently, refusal to allow the deduction of child care expenses did not constitute indirect discrimination. Child care is a special need which does not come within Article 3(1). In both cases the court rejected the Advocate General's plea for a wider interpretation of Article 3(1).

Equal treatment principle
Article 4 (1) defines the equal treatment principle as being no discrimination whatsoever on grounds of sex either directly, or indirectly by reference in particular to marital or family status. It also sets out some examples of areas where the principle applies.

Direct effect of the equal treatment principle
It was held in *Netherlands v Federatie Nederlandse Vakbeweging* (1986) that Article 4(1) had direct effect.

The direct effect of Article 4(1) means that the discriminatory effects of earlier provisions of national law cannot extend beyond the implementation date (*Borrie Clarke v Chief Adjudication Officer* (1987)). In order to comply with the directive the UK abolished a discriminatory invalidity pension and replaced it with an allowance, which was non -

discriminatory. Recipients of the old benefit were automatically entitled to the new benefit.

The applicant prior to the implementation date was denied benefit when it would have been granted to a man in the same situation. She contended that she was automatically entitled to the new benefit. The ECJ held that she was so entitled.

Similar problems arose in *Dik v College van Burgemeester en Wethouders te Arnhem et al* case 80/87; the applicants failed to obtain unemployment benefit before the implementation date, as they could not satisfy discriminatory criteria. The Dutch government still refused to provide the benefit after the implementation date. Again it was held that the direct effect of Article 4(1) made any discriminatory provision illegal as from the implementation date, including an earlier provision that had effects after that date.

Indirect discrimination

In *Teuling* (1988) the applicant was able to claim from a Dutch social insurance scheme for invalided workers. Initially, the benefits took no account of personal circumstances and recipients were entitled to at least the equivalent of the minimum wage.

After reforms to the law, the applicant was only entitled to 70% of the minimum wage as her husband's earnings were taken into account. To qualify for benefit which was 100% of the minimum wage she would have to have a dependent family. She claimed that the law was discriminatory, as many more men have dependents than women, therefore, the changes had a greater impact on women than on men.

The ECJ held that provisions that were indirectly discriminatory would be illegal unless it could be shown that they could be justified on grounds other than sex. In this case, additional supplements were paid to claimants with dependants, as they had a greater burden and would otherwise fall below the poverty line. The supplement was intended to prevent claimants from falling into destitution and were therefore justified.

The case is revealing about the ECJ's approach. They are prepared to accept a 'levelling down'. The supplement was denied to both women and men where there were alternative sources of income. This is non-discriminatory but it does not improve the position of women and worsens the position of some men.

In *Ruzius-Wilbrink v Bestuur van de Bedrijfsvereniging voor Overheidsdiensten* (1987) it was held that there was no objective justification for treating the entitlement to invalidity benefit of part time workers differently from full time workers.

It can be seen that the ECJ is far less interfering in defining what constitutes objective justification in social security cases than in employment cases. This could be explained on policy grounds. Rulings in social security cases can have widespread financial implications for the governments of Member States.

Exceptions

Article 7 (1) expressly allows Member States to exclude certain matters from the scope of the equal treatment principle, including *inter alia* at para (a) the determination of pensionable age for the purposes of old age and retirement pensions and possible consequences thereof for other benefits.

It was held in *The Queen v Secretary of State for Social Security* (1992) that Article 7(1) could justify inequality with respect to the number of contributions required to be paid in order to obtain a full retirement pension. Men could be made to contribute for 44 years and women for 39 years and still receive the same benefit.

The Member States are under an obligation to keep the exceptions under review, in the light of social developments under Article 7(2).

Although *prima facie* the exceptions are 'women friendly' as they preserve certain privileges for women, they have been criticised by Prechal and Burrows as reinforcing the traditional family model of 'breadwinner husband' and dependant wife, which creates less of an incentive for women to become financially independent.

Equal treatment in occupational social security schemes

Unlike statutory social security schemes, private occupational schemes do come within Article 119 (*Worringham and Humphreys*) and (*Barber*). The decision in *Barber* has, therefore, curtailed the application of this Directive but it is still of use in respect of indirect discrimination, where Article 119 is of limited application.

Article 2(1) states that 'occupational social security schemes' are schemes which are not governed by the social security Directive (79/7) and whose purpose is to provide employed or self employed persons with benefits intended to supplement benefits provided by statutory social security schemes or to replace them, whether membership of such schemes is compulsory or optional. Article 2(2) provides a list of exceptions.

With a few exceptions Directive 86/378 is enacted in very similar terms to Directive 79/7. It applies to the same categories of persons (Article 3) in respect of the same risks (Article 4). The difference is that Directive 86/378 does not exclude family or survivors' benefits provided these benefits form part of the consideration paid by the employer by reason of the employee's employment.

Equal treatment in self employment

Many women in self employment face difficulties because their status is unclear. Women working in a family business often fall between the two stools of being considered neither a partner nor an employee. This can prejudice their access to welfare benefits, vocational training and representation on trade bodies. An important function of this Directive is not only to implement the equal treatment principle to the self employed but also to make the status of spouses who help in family businesses clearer.

Accordingly, Article 2 provides that the directive applies to (a) self employed workers, ie persons pursuing a gainful activity for their own account, including farmers and members of the liberal professions and (b) their spouses, not being employees or partners, where they habitually participate in the activities of the self employed worker and perform the same tasks or ancillary tasks. Paragraph (b) expressly includes workers such as farmers' spouses and shopkeepers' spouses who traditionally have suffered from uncertain status.

Protocol on social policy

Annexed to the Treaty on European Union is a protocol on social policy. The UK secured an opt out to the agreement attached to the protocol which was concluded amongst the other 11 Member States.

Article 2 of the protocol provides that the Community shall support and complement the activities of the Member States in the field of, *inter alia*, equality between men and women with regard to labour market opportunities and treatment at work.

Article 6 paras 1 and 2 are virtually identical to Article 119. Article 6 para 3 allows for positive discrimination in favour of women (see above Article 2(4) equal treatment Directive).

The legal effect of the UK opt out is unclear. As stated above one of the objectives of sex equality legislation is to create fair competition. An opt out will distort competition if one Member State is under a less onerous burden than the others.

There is also uncertainty as to whether the agreement constitutes an intergovernmental agreement between the 11 States or a form of Community law which is only binding on 11 States. There are misgivings about both approaches as they would equally undermine the uniformity of Community law.

The Agreement annexed to the Social Protocol refers to the Council adopting Directives, in order to implement decisions taken under the Agreement. However, it is thought by Curtin 30 (1993) CMLRev 17 that this type of act will not be the same as Directives, as defined by Article 189.

If Directives are found to be intergovernmental agreements which are to be implemented at national level then individuals will face difficulties in upholding their rights through enforcement actions and actions for judicial review.

Although the concept of a 'two speed' Community is new, what is different is under the opt out where Member States share different aims.

Although the Protocol talks of the 11 Member States 'borrowing' the Community institutions in order to take decisions relating to the agreement, it is uncertain whether the ECJ is a 'borrowed' institution. If the ECJ is outside the scope of the agreement then this has an adverse effect on individual rights because of the difficulties facing individuals in bringing actions for judicial review. This is a particularly potent threat to the effectiveness of the agreement, as the expansion of the Community's social policy has been primarily brought about by decisions of the ECJ based on actions brought by individuals.

Even if the ECJ is not a 'borrowed' institution for the purposes of the Social Policy Agreement, Szyszczak in *Legal Issues of the Maastricht Treaty* argues that it can still be used to test the legality of Directives brought under the Agreement. The Social Protocol says that it does not affect the *acquis communautaire*. A Social Policy Agreement Directive could be reviewed by the ECJ on the basis that it does not comply with the *acquis communautaire*.

Furthermore, there are likely to be disputes as to the relationship between the Agreement and other Community competences, particularly Article 118a. Eleven Member States wish to minimise recourse to the Agreement and use other Treaty Articles which bind the UK, whereas the UK wish to do the opposite. Challenges will be made to the legal bases of legislation brought under Article 118a in the form of actions for annulment under Article 173, which will be heard by the ECJ. This has already happened in relation to the Working Hours Directive.

Barber protocol

A protocol annexed to the TEU attempts to interpret the decision in *Barber v Guardian Royal Exchange Assurance Group* (1990) (see above) so that it applies only to benefits under occupational social security schemes to periods of employment after 17 May 1990.

Pressure for the inclusion of this protocol came from the powerful UK and Dutch pension lobbies and consequently it has been cited as an example of the influence vested rights had in the outcome of the TEU, at the expense of individual rights.

There is uncertainty as to whether the Member States intended to amend Article 119 or interpret Article 119. If their intention was the latter then the Member States' interpretation accords with that given by the ECJ in *Ten Oever* (1993).

Harvey in *Legal Issues of the Maastricht Treaty* makes the following criticisms of the protocol:

- it interferes with the institutional balance of the Communities as the Member States have usurped the function of the ECJ;
- it interferes with the separation of powers in the Community and consequently, the rule of law;
- it delays full implementation of the equal treatment principle and denies a human right, the right to equality;
- the protocol may conflict with the *acquis communautaire* because of a combination of the above.

Critique of the equal treatment principle

Despite the introduction of equality legislation, women still lag behind men in the earnings league. Dworkin distinguishes between the right to equal treatment and the right to treatment as an equal. The former is the right to the same distribution of opportunities, resources or burdens whereas the latter is the right to be treated with the same respect and concern as anyone else. The equal treatment standard is the standard adopted by the Community. Prechal and Burrows identify the following shortcomings with this approach:

- it presupposes that women always have a man to compare themselves to;
- it does not guarantee an overall raising of standards but can lead to a levelling down in certain areas men and women need special and different rights;

- it ignores the differences in the roles of men and women according to their culturally defined positions and most importantly, it does not take into account unequal distribution of household and domestic commitments.

Revision Notes

EC law on sex discrimination

- Article 119 lays down a general principle of equal pay for equal work;
- Protocol and agreement on social policy annexed to the TEU (UK opt out);
- Protocol on the decision in *Barber v Guardian Royal Exchange Assurance Group* (1990) annexed to the TEU;
- General principle of equality;
- Directive 75/117 equal pay for work of equal value;
- Directive 76/207 provides for equal treatment for men and women in the context of employment;
- Directive 79/9 equal treatment for matters of social security;
- Directive 86/378 equal treatment for occupational pension schemes;
- Directive 86/613 equal treatment in self employment;
- Directive 92/85 maternity Directive.

Dual objectives of sex equality legislation

It was held in *Defrenne (No 2)* (1976) that Article 119 had a 'dual objective' this was economic and social.

Direct and indirect discrimination

Direct discrimination can be defined as similar situations being treated differently or different situations being treated alike. It is always illegal unless it comes within one of the permitted derogations but even then it must satisfy the principle of proportionality (*Johnston* (1986)).

Indirect discrimination refers to neutral (non discriminatory) criteria which have a greater adverse impact on one sex compared to the other. A common example are provisions which adversely effect part time workers. There is nothing overtly discriminatory about inferior treatment for part time workers until it is remembered that the vast majority of part time are women. There is no absolute principle prohibiting indirect discrimination and measures will be legal where they are 'objectively justified' (*Jenkins* (1980))(ie there is some valid, non-discriminatory reason for them) provided that they satisfy the principle of proportionality by:

- meeting a genuine need of the enterprise;
- being suitable action for attaining the objective set;
- being necessary for the purpose which was being attained (*Bilka-Kaufhaus* (1986)).

The onus is on the employer to show that the measures are objectively justified (*Danfoss* (1989)).

It is for the national court to decide whether the measures are objectively justified and whether they satisfy the principle of proportionality. Having said that the ECJ has given some guidance as to what they consider to be 'objective justification':

- justification based on a 'genuine objective of social policy' (*Rinner-Kühn* (1989));
- differentials based on market forces necessitating higher pay to attract suitable candidates, if need and proportionality are proved (*Enderby* (1993));
- the need to lighten the administrative, legal and financial burden on small employers (*Kirsammer-Hack* (1993)).

Equal pay

Article 119

Direct effect of Article 119

Article 119 has both vertical and horizontal direct effect (*Defrenne (No 2)* (1976)) but there is a limit to the extent it can be relied on for indirect discrimination.

Meaning of 'pay'

The term 'pay' has been given a wide definition for the purposes of Article 119. The advantage of this is that it has extended the possible range of actions that can be brought under the Treaty and minimised recourse to the Directives, which do not have horizontal direct effect. The following have been held to be 'pay' by the ECJ:

- statutory sick pay (*Rinner-Kühn* (1989));
- differences in pay caused by separate collective bargaining processes which an employer is unable to show are objectively justified (*Enderby* (1993);
- contributions to 'contracted out' (privatised) pension schemes (*Worringham* (1981), *Barber* (1990));

- statutory redundancy payments (*Barber*);
- statutory redundancy payments to workers over 60 (*Commission v Belgium* (1993));
- statutory and occupational redundancy payments (*Barber*);
- *ex gratia* payments (*Barber*);
- different retirement ages for men and women under an occupational pension scheme (*Barber*);
- pensions paid under a trust (*Coloroll* (1994));
- transferees to a pension scheme from another pension scheme where Article 119 has not been observed (*Coloroll*);
- right of part time workers to join a pension scheme, unless there is an 'objective justification' for their exclusion (*Vroege* (1994));
- benefits granted in respect of employment and not as a result of a contractual obligation (*Garland* (1982));
- differences in pay between full and part time workers unless they can be 'objectively justified' (*Jenkins* (1981)) and satisfy the principle of proportionality (*Bilka-Kaufhaus* (1986)).

Article 119 does not apply to the following:

- compulsory State social security schemes which apply to occupational branches (*Defrenne (No 1)* (1971) (see above for the list of exceptions to this rule);
- the conditions of employment (*Defrenne (No 3)* (1978));
- additional voluntary contributions (*Coloroll*);
- single sex pension schemes (*Coloroll*);
- the reduction in level of benefits of advantaged class to level of disadvantaged class (*Coloroll*);
- the differences in retirement ages in relation to occupational pensions between men and women before 17 May 1990 (*Ten Oever* (1993), protocol to the TEU);
- the basis on which pensions were calculated before 17 May 1990 (*Neath* (1993));
- the right of part timers to join a pension fund before 8 April 1976 (*Vroege* (1994)).

Meaning of equal work

- Do not have to be contemporaneously employed with comparator (*Macarthys v Smith* (1980)).
- Cannot use a hypothetical male as a comparator (*Macarthys*).
- Can compare with comparators on different earnings (*Murphy v An Bord Telecom Eireann* (1987)).

Equal pay Directive

Article 1 of the Directive is said to restate Article 119. Recourse will be made to the Directive where discrimination can only be identified by additional criteria eg a job evaluation scheme.

Comparison can be made with work of equal value in different establishments covered by the same collective agreement (*Commission v Denmark* case 143/83).

Criteria such as muscular effort can be used in a job evaluation scheme provided the system as a whole precludes discrimination and the criteria used are objectively justified (*Rummler v Dato-Druck GmbH* (1987)).

Criteria such as 'seniority' and 'flexibility' can be taken into account, subject to restrictions (*Danfoss* (1989)).

Equality of treatment

Equality of treatment Directive

Male and female workers must receive equal treatment in access to employment, vocational training and promotion.

Equality of access

Equality of access to employment
If an applicant is actually pregnant, dismissal on grounds of pregnancy will be illegal (*Dekker* (1991), (*Webb* (1994)).

If a worker is no longer pregnant but is suffering from a long term illness connected with pregnancy then dismissal will only be illegal if the applicant has suffered adverse treatment compared to a male employee suffering from a long term illness (*Aldi* (1990)).

Equality of access to vocational training
Vocational training can be offered to a group of workers who are predominantly male, if there is an objective reason for doing so (*Danfoss* (1989)).

Equality of working conditions

Conditions governing dismissal
Article 5 provides that working conditions include dismissal. Access to a voluntary redundancy scheme comes within Article 5, unless it is linked to statutory retirement age (*Burton* (1982)).

Where retirement age is calculated for any reason other than eligibility for State pension then it comes within Article 5 (*Marshall* (1984), *Beets-Proper* (1986)).

Adoption leave
Adoption leave is not a working condition (*Commission v Italy* (1983)).

Derogations from equal treatment principle
All derogations from the equal treatment principle must be interpreted strictly and are subject to the proportionality principle (*Johnston* (1986)).

Where sex is the determining factor
Where the sex of the worker is a determining factor then derogation are permitted from the equal treatment principle. This includes:

* biological differences;
* social or cultural differences;
* environment (*Johnston*).

Member States are under an obligation to draw up a list of excluded occupations, which is reviewable by the Commission.

Exclusions can only be for specific activities and general/blanket bans are forbidden (*Commission v UK* (1983); *Commission v France* (1986); *Johnston*)).

Permitted discrimination at lower levels may necessitate having to discriminate at higher echelons even though sex may not be the determining factor at the higher grade (*Commission v France* (1986)).

Protection of women, in particular with regard to pregnancy and maternity
Measures invoked under this section must involve a risk specific to women (*Johnston*). There is no precise definition of maternity (*Hofmann* (1984)) but it does not extend to mothers of school age children (*Commission v France* (1989)).

Effective remedies
Member States are under an obligation to provide effective remedies where there has been a breach of the equal treatment principle (*Von Colson* (1984), *Harz* (1984) and *Marshall (No 2)* (1993)) which includes effective procedural remedies (*Emmott* (1991)).

Social security Directive

The Directive only applies to the 'working population' but a wide definition has been given to this and it includes someone who has interrupted work to look after an invalid relative (*Drake* (1985)) but not someone who has given up work to look after children and is unable to resume were through illness, unless actively looking for work (*Johnson* (1991)) nor does it include anyone never engaged in paid work (*Achterberg* (1989)).

Exceptions to the principle are contained in Article 7(1) and include determination of pensionable age for old age and retirement pensions.

Occupational social security scheme Directive

The application of this directive has been curtailed as a result of the ruling in *Barber* (1990) which held that Article 119 applies to occupational pensions (unlike State pensions which are outside Article 119). The Directive is only of use in relation to some types of indirect discrimination. The Directive is drafted in very similar terms to the social security Directive with the important difference that it includes family and survivors' benefits.

Self employment Directive

An important function of this Directive is to extend the equal treatment principle not only to the self employed but also to their spouses.

Opt outs

UK opt out from Agreement on Social Policy

A number of legal issues have been raised by the UK opt out from the Agreement on Social Policy, annexed to the Social Policy Protocol:

- Does it affect the *acquis communautaire* by undermining the principles of unity and reciprocity on which the EC Treaty is based?
- What is the status of the agreement? Does it simply have the status of an intergovernmental agreement? Are Directives brought under the agreement the same as those under Article 189?
- Is the ECJ a 'borrowed' Institution?

Barber protocol

There is a further protocol purporting to explain the temporal basis of the ECJ's decision in *Barber* (1990).

Index